NAVAJO
AND
HOPI DYES

ISBN 1-883736-08-0

PRINTED IN THE UNITED STATES OF AMERICA

Bill Rieske
HISTORIC INDIAN PUBLISHERS
1404 Sunset Drive
P.O. Box 16074
Salt Lake City, Utah 84116-0074

Table of Contents

Publishers Statement

Publisher's Statement

It is especially satisfying to publish this combined book of Navajo and Hopi Dyes. Since 1973 I have devoted my time to research and publishing educational material on Indian history and Indian studies. In 1974 I was able to buy the Navajo Dye Source shown on the cover of this book. The artist-designer is unknown. The poster from this dye source is a popular item. The 27 specimens shown were the largest variety I had seen, up to that time. Our latest purchase has 60 specimens. The Navajo Native Dye Appendix, following the Navajo section, shows the number of specimens displayed on the two sources. These native dyes continue to hold worldwide interest. The contrast of Navajo and Hopi uses continues to be seen in this combined book. Both booklets were originally published to preserve the traditional methods and recipes for the tribal members.

Permission to publish the Hopi Dyes was granted by the Museum of Northern Arizona, holder of the copyright. Permission was also granted to make some additions to the original work. Common names have been added, leaving the Hopi words as they were in the original editions.

The Navajo section is published without any changes. The Navajo Appendix A follows the original booklet and is a separate copyrighted work.

Enjoy these traditional and authentic recipes and methods from two great nations in the great southwest.

Bill Rieske

NAVAJO NATIVE DYES

Their Preparation and Use

Recipes formulated by
NONABAH G. BRYAN, Navajo
Instructor in Weaving

Compiled by
STELLA YOUNG
Head, Home Economics Department
Wingate Vocational High School

Illustrated by
CHARLES KEETSIE SHIRLEY, Navajo

Originally Published 1940 by the U.S. Bureau of Indian Affairs
ISBN 0-910584-49-4
PRINTED IN THE UNITED STATES OF AMERICA

CONTENTS

INTRODUCTION

With the introduction of sheep into the Southwest by the Spaniards in the latter half of the sixteenth century, wool became a fiber accessible to the Navajo. Contact with the Pueblo Indians introduced him to the upright loom. Navajo genius discovered that the plants and minerals of his desert home could be used to change his native white and black wool to a multitude of soft and lustrous colors. Blended on the upright loom, these produced the antique Navajo rugs so much prized for their simplicity in design, which consists for the most part of variations of simple stripes, and for their colors—the pale yellows, browns, grays, tans, and rose, which reflect the beauty of the desert.

Recognizing the unique achievements of these ancient art-craftsmen and desiring to perpetuate their art, the Home Economics Department at the Wingate Vocational High School undertook in 1934 to revive interest in native dyed rugs by discovering how these native dyes were obtained. This bulletin is a record of the research and experimentation carried on in the course of the study.

The department was fortunate in having on its staff Mrs. Nonabah G. Bryan, a Navajo woman, educated in government schools, and familiar with the reservation, having spent most of her life on it. She was employed to teach Navajo weaving, at which she had become an artist. Much of her effort was spent in perfecting native dyes. She used in the process only those materials procurable from the reservation. Her foundation recipes are largely those of her ancestors—making of black dye by mixing the m i n e r a l yellow ocher with pitch from the piñon (*Pinus edulis*) and dyewater from the three leaved sumac (*Rhus trilobata*) and obtaining yellows and browns by the boiling of certain plants with raw alum or water from juniper ashes (*Juniperus monosperma*). But the dyeing of rose yarn by fermenting prickly pear cactus fruit (*Opuntia polycantha*), and the making of green by first dyeing the yarn yellow with sagebrush (*Artemisia tridentata*) and later putting it in a black afterbath dyewater, are her own discoveries.

At the beginning of the study only standard plants were used, but as the work progressed, a wide variety was utilized in the hope that Indians from all parts of the reservation could find satisfactory products close enough to their homes to make this method of dyeing practicable. Many new shades and tints have been developed t h r o u g h experimentation with different plant combinations as well as by varying the recipes used for dyeing with the same plant.

The yellows are the easiest of all to obtain and range from clear y e l l o w through green yellows to mustard. The browns may be light or dark and often have considerable red, rose, or purple in them. The black made from the mineral ocher, pitch from the piñon (*Pinus edulis*), and the three-leaved sumac (*Rhus trilobata*), is bluish-black and is quite d i f f e r e n t from the brown-black of the natural black sheep. Tans, grays, orange, pinks, and rose appear frequently in native dyed rugs. A good green was never obtained in ancient times from strictly reservation materials. The yarn was first dyed yellow and then boiled in indigo blue to make the desired shade or tint of green. Indigo was obtained by the Indians through trade with Mexico. Some very yellow-greens have been made from plants grown locally. The Denver Museum of Art, Indian Leaflet Series No. 74, states that the bark and b e r r i e s of the one-seeded juniper (*Juniperus monosperma*) are used for dyeing wool green; in the Fort Wingate experiments, however, the bast and sprigs of the one-seeded j u n i p e r have yielded only an orange-tan and a yellow-tan (p. 39 of the present publication). In 1936 Mrs. Bryan discovered an interesting process for making green by dyeing yarn yellow with sagebrush (*Artemisia tridentata*), or orange with Navajo tea (*Telemsperma gracile*), and then boiling this in the afterbath dyewater from native black dye (pp. 64, 65, and 70). By this method a number of interesting shades and tints can be obtained. These native dyes were combined with cream, gray, brown, and brown-black of the natural wool.

The old Navajo had no exact measurements and even today on the reservation only approximate measures are used. Cactus fruit, plants and the barks of various trees are measured in pans, sumac and Navajo tea are made into rolls, rugs are so many hand-lengths in size. Sufficient supplies of either wool or dye materials were seldom on hand so they used what they had. If, in the early spring, the supply of wool was depleted, a strip a few inches wide was sheared along either side of the backbone of the sheep. More could not be taken lest the animal die of cold. For these reasons every rug was an experiment. If there was an insufficiency of warp or woof yarn for a large rug a small one was made instead and the design modified to fit it. If the supply of mountain mahogany root bark ran out, ground lichens might be substituted or several plants mixed

6

together to approximate the desired color. A rug had to be made to be traded for necessary food.

As the Navajo of today is trained to accumulate supplies for a year in advance, planned rugs may now be woven. The craftsman will continue to create the design and work out the color scheme for the individual rug as in times past. Exactitude in the making of rugs is now a possibility and the weaver need not be curtailed in the accomplishment of her dream by the necessity of substituting what she has for what she would like to have.

It is now becoming possible to use exact recipes for dyes on the reservation. It has been the purpose of the Home Economics Department of the Wingate Vocational High School to assist in discovering methods which are practical and in formulating recipes for dyes made entirely from reservation products. Those so formulated up to March 1935 were published at that time in a mimeographed bulletin by the school. This new publication also includes those which have been developed since then.

A number of books have already been written on this subject. The justification for this present publication lies in the fact that it contains definitely formulated recipes, and that recipes developed through our own experimentation are included.

Working with Mrs. Bryan through this series of experiments has been a pleasure and profitable experience.

Grateful acknowledgment is given to the following people for their generous help during the preparation of this bulletin. To Mr. Herman Bogard, Superintendent of the Wingate Vocational High School, and to Mr. Leroy F. Jackson, former Superintendent of the school, for their generous cooperation which has made this study possible; to Dr. Ruth Underhill, Associate Supervisor of Indian Education (Anthropologist), for assistance in editing the bulletin; to Dr. E. F. Castetter, Professor of Botany and to Mr. Francis H. Elmore, of the University of New Mexico for the botanical classification of the dye plants; to Dr. John D. Clark, Professor of Chemistry at the University of New Mexico, for the chemical analysis and classification of the rocks used; to Father Berard Haile of Gallup and to Dr. John P. Harrington of the Smithsonian Institution for the Navajo names for the plants and minerals used; to Mr. Charles Keetsie Shirley, illustrator for the Navajo Service, for the drawings of the dye plants; and to all others who have in any way contributed to the experimental study or to the writing of the bulletin.

Ft. Wingate, New Mexico, 1939   *Stella Young*
Wingate Vocational High School

MRS. BRYAN DYES YARN FOR A RUG

Mrs. Bryan decides to dye some yarns for a native-dye rug. She plans to use a brown made from mountain mahogany root bark (*Cercocarpus montanus*), rose from prickly pear cactus fruit (*Opunta polycantha*), green from sagebrush (*Artemisia tridentata*) and black afterbath dyewater, black from ocher, piñon pitch (*Pinus edulis*) and three-leaved sumac (*Rhus trilobata*), and white from cream-colored wool whitened with gypsum.

From her store of supplies she selects the materials which she has gathered one by one at the proper season during the past year. From the mountains she has dug mountain mahogany root in the early fall, at which time they give the strongest color. As soon as they were dug she pounded the bark from them and dried it. The last of September she traveled to the nearest mesa where she knew from experience a bed of prickly pear grew. She picked the red fruit, rubbed it in the sand to remove the thorns, and carried it home and dried it. She went twenty-five miles to a coal mine where she gathered her year's supply of ocher.   Having found it at this place the year before, she was quite sure she could do it again. She knew a spot in the foothills of the mountains where there was a great deal of pitch on the piñon trees.   She gathered cans full of it one day as she passed the place on her way home from a squaw dance.   She took down several rolls of dried sumac which she had gathered the summer before from the arroyo at the back of the Wingate school. Sagebrush was no problem because it grew all around her, stayed green all winter, and only required picking. She gathered the whitener, gypsum, where she had found it many times before in some shale near a coal deposit.

As she checked over her supplies the only things she lacked were her mordants. The raw alum was in a can where it had been placed as she gathered it from under certain large rocks found in the flat reservation country.   The one-seeded juniper (*Juniperus monosperma*) twigs she gathers fresh from the foothills of the mountains just back of her home the evening before she needs them.

She has been carding and spinning her warp and woof yarns for several weeks. Her wool has been shorn from sheep which produce a high quality blanket wool. For this reason it has not been necessary for her to wash it before carding, because it contains little grease and picks up a minimum of dirt. She has, h o w e v e r, shaken it well and spread it on the sand, s h o r n side up, and sprinkled it with white clay which she had previously gathered in certain arid regions in the Navajo country. As the sun heats the grease, the clay absorbs it. After shaking it again thoroughly, she cards it. Now that she has her yarn spun she washes it before she dyes it.

She takes from her supplies, some soap weed (*Yucca baccata*) which she dug one day while out on the mesa. She had already crushed the root, heated it over hot coals and dried it so that it would keep indefinitely.   Now that she is ready to use it she rubs some of it in cold w a t e r until there is a heavy l a t h e r. Before beginning, she is careful to free her hands and the tub of oil or grease, otherwise, the root would produce no lather. After removing the soap weed, she adds hot water to make it comfortably warm for washing.   She sudses the yarn up and down, but is careful not to rub or twist it, because she doesn't want it to get lumpy. When it is clean, she rinses it thoroughly and hangs it up to dry.

With yarn clean and dye materials assembled, she is ready to do the actual dyeing. The rose yarn is dyed first, because it takes a week or sometimes two to complete the process. She selects an enamel kettle for dyeing, because she found that if she does it in tin or aluminum the acid developed in the dyebath while fermenting reacts upon the metal, and the color of the dye is changed. She measures out the dried prickly pear fruit and covers it with lukewarm water to soak overnight. In the morning she mashes it well, strains it, and adds enough more cool water to cover the yarn completely. She then places the wet yarn in it, rubs the dye into it well, covers it, and sets it in a warm place to ferment, having learned from previous experience that if she boils it the lovely rose color will change to tan. Many times each day during the following week she rubs the dye into the yarn. If she finds at the end of the time that the rose color is not as deep as she wishes it, she puts it in another dyebath of the same strength as before and allows it to ferment another week. She then rinses it thoroughly and hangs it up to dry.

The black yarn, which she dyes next, is the most difficult of all to prepare. She first puts the sumac on to boil. Then she grinds the chunks of ocher between Navajo grinding stones to a fine powder and toasts it to cocoa brown in a frying-pan, after which she adds the piñon pitch, a little at a time, stirring it constantly. It smokes and smarts her eyes, throat, and nose, but she continues to stir it until this smoke has all passed off. During this heating process, the pitch has reduced the iron in the ocher to a ferrous compound. She lets it cool until just lukewarm and then adds it to the sumac dyebath water which she has previously strained from the twigs. The tannin in the sumac water unites with the ferrous compound in the ocher and pitch mixture and makes black ink. She stirs the dyebath well and notes there is a sufficient quantity so the yarn can float in it. She lets it boil a few minutes then adds the wet yarn. She prefers to use the natural black yarn as it dyes black more easily. She stirs this well as she desires to distribute the dye evenly into all parts of the wool. After it has boiled for two or three hours, she takes the kettle from the stove and leaves the yarn in the dyebath overnight, because she thinks this makes a faster dye. In the morning she rinses it two or three times, or until the color ceases to run out into the water, and hangs it up to dry.

She plans to do the green yarn next, because she is going to use the dyewater left over from the black dye. She calls this the afterbath dyewater. She first dyes the yarn yellow with the sagebrush, then boils it in the afterbath dyewater to give the final green color. Again she selects an enamel vessel for dyeing, because she wants a clear bright yellow when it is finished; if she had wished to have a mustard yellow she would have used a tin or aluminum kettle. She weighs the sagebrush, adds the water, and boils it for about two hours, after which she strains out the twigs and adds the raw alum, which she has thrown on hot coals until it started to foam. This she stirs well and boils a few minutes, then adds her wet yarn, stirring as she adds it to be sure that it takes the dye evenly. She boils it about three hours and then lifts it out into the black afterbath dyewater which she has brought to a boil. She stirs this well and boils it two hours longer, then lets it stay in the dyebath overnight. In the morning she rinses it and hangs it up to dry.

She dyes her brown yarn just as she did her yellow, except that she uses juniper ash water for her mordant, instead of raw alum. Just before she is ready to add this to the dyebath, she sets fire to a big handful of juniper branches, burning only the green needles, and holds them over a frying pan so that the ashes will fall into it. Then she adds boiling water which, after straining, she uses as a mordant with mountain mahogany root bark.

The white yarn is the last prepared. She throws the crystal rock of gypsum on the coals until it turns white, and, after it cools, she grinds it to a powder between Navajo grinding stones. She then measures it and stirs it into the water and rinses her natural creamed-colored yarn in the solution. When it dries, it will be much whiter, because the gypsum forms a film over the wool.

With her supply of yarn, Mrs. Bryan is now ready to do her weaving. The finished rugs sells by weight and commands a higher price than a rug of equal weight made from undyed or analine dyed wool. Much more time and effort have gone into the preparation of the yarn, and the total effect of these soft, lustrous colors blended in a simple design make an art product that is sought by buyers in spite of the greater cost.

ADDITIONAL OBSERVATIONS REGARDING NATIVE DYES

Dyeing with native dyes is slow and arduous as shown by the above description. Many laws of chemistry are involved in the process but the facts were discovered by the Navajo through trial and error. A number of interesting observations, not included in the above discussion, have been made during the experiments and are listed below:

1. The same species of plant grown in different sections of the country may give different shades of color. The shade of color may also vary from year to year from a plant grown in the same locality.

2. All dye plants may be used with or without a mordant. The use of a mordant deepens the color and occasionally changes it. The use of a different mordant, or varying the quantity of mordant used, also produces a difference in the color given by the same plant. Colors dyed without a mordant are reasonably fast.

3. Longer boiling of the dye with the yarn usually produces a deeper color. Occasionally the color is entirely changed.

4. Allowing the yarn to remain in the dyebath overnight deepens and brightens the color. It is believed that it also produces a faster color.

5. It is necessary that most of the dyes be boiled with the yarn to produce the color. There are exceptions to this, however. Cactus fruit, some berries, and flowers lose their color when boiled. For this reason we allow the dye to ferment into the yarn as explained in the recipes.

6. The afterbath yarn, or the second yarn dyed in the same dyewater, is a softer, lighter tint of the same color.

7. Most of the plants may be used either fresh or dried. Fresh plants are usually stronger than when dried. Therefore, less of the fresh is required

to produce the same color. Dried canyaigre root, however, is stronger than when it is fresh. One must bear this in mind when substituting in the following recipes.

8. Dried barks, plants, and fruits should be soaked overnight before using.

9. Yarns must be rinsed several times after dyeing to remove the unabsorbed dye.

10. The yarns dyed by the following recipes have been tested for color fastness when treated with commercial cleaners and moth preventives and were found to be unchanged by them.

PREPARING WOOL

Wool must be cleaned before carding. It may be either dry-cleaned or washed with either of the two occurrent soapplant species, narrow-leaf soap-plant, Spanish amole, tsa'aszi'ooz *(Yucca gluaca)*, or wide-leaf soap-plant, Spanish popularly látil, dictionary Spanish látil, tsa'aszi'ntxyeelih *(Yucca baccata)*. Wool which is dry-cleaned before carding makes a smoother yarn than that which is washed, and so all of it that is not too dirty is treated this way. The coarse dirt and much of the grease is removed during this process.

TO DRY-CLEAN WOOL

Spread the fleece in the sun, either on brush, rocks or sand, shorn (cut) side up. Shake while spreading it. In addition, sprinkle it with white clay or toasted pulverized gypsum. (These two materials and their methods of preparation are described under "Whitening Wool.") After a thorough sunning shake until dirt falls out.

TO WASH YARN

It is necessary that yarn be clean before it is dyed. For this reason it is washed after spinning and before dyeing. The only soap which the ancient Navajo knew was obtained from the two soapweeds above mentioned. The roots of these yuccas contain the compound saponin and make an excellent soap which is still preferred to the commercial article for washing wool.

Látil and amole are sword-leaved plants and grow about two feet high. The former has a wide blade and the latter a narrow one. Látil grows commonly throughout the reservation between 4,500 and 8,000 feet altitude and amole from 3,000 to 7,500 feet.

Both may be used either fresh or dried and may be dug at anytime of year when there is not too much frost in the ground. Amole root is simply dug and crushed and dried in the sun if it is to be kept for any length of time. Látil is treated in the same way, except that it is heated well over hot coals or a stove after being crushed and before it is dried or used fresh. Heating in this way produces a better lather.

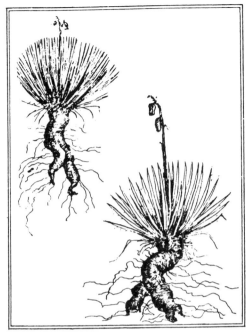

AMOLE AND LATIL

Látil is stronger and is preferred by many for washing wool.

If one washes white and light colored yarns with either of the two soap-plants, the yarns do not absorb the grease from the weavers' hands, but when soap is used for the entire washing without a finishing rinse in soap-plant suds, the yarns absorb oil from the weavers' hands and become soiled in appearance.

TO WASH YARN WITH YUCCA ROOT

1   handful crushed yucca root (fresh or dried)
1   quart cold water
Sufficient hot water to wash the yarn
1   pound yarn

Free hands and tub from grease as yucca roots will not lather when grease is present.

Rub the crushed roots between the hands in the cold water until there is a heavy lather. Strain. Add enough hot water to make a warm solution. Wash the yarn thoroughly, using a second suds water if necessary to clean it. Rinse twice.

The finest yarn is washed after spinning. But if the wool is very dirty it must be done before carding. In that case great care must be taken not to twist or press it hard as this felts the wool and makes it form lumps. It must be floated around loosely in the water and removed carefully (not wrung) and placed on screens, boards, rocks, or sand to drain and dry.

MIXED NATURAL WOOL COLORS

Lovely black (brown-black), tan, brown, and cream colors can be obtained naturally from various colored sheep.

GRAY

¼ pound black wool
¾ pound cream wool

Mix black and cream wool together and card. Pull to pieces, mix again and card again to get even color. The proportion of black used will determine the resulting shade of gray.

BROWN

½ pound natural brown wool
½ pound natural tan wool

Prepare same as for "gray" wool. This makes a very pleasing shade of brown.

TAN

½ pound natural brown wool
½ pound natural cream colored wool

Prepare as for "Gray" wool.

WHITENING WOOL

½ cup white clay (dleesh), or 2 tablespoons ground, toasted gypsum (selenite variety) (tseső).
2 cups water.
1 pound yarn (natural cream color).

Dissolve the clay or the gypsum in the water and rinse the yarn in it. This will make a white rather than a cream yarn.

So-called white clay is mostly a marl (calcium carbonate). It is found in arid regions throughout the Navajo country as a vein around the tablelands. The Indians have definite places where they dig it.

Gypsum of the selenite variety is found in small quanities here and there in some shales associated with coal deposits in New Mexico. The Navajo pick it up aound coal mines. It has a crystalline appearance. It is toasted by throwing it into the fire or baking it in the oven until it turns white. It is ground into a fine powder between Navajo grinding stones before using.

MORDANTS

ASHES OF JUNIPER   (JUNIPERUS MONOSPERMA)

gad bididze' doo bilatxahi bileeshch'iih bitxoo'

The Navajo commonly, but mistakenly, call this juniper cedar. It is also called desert or one-seeded juniper. It is an evergreen tree which grows five feet and higher, depending upon the amount of moisture. It grows plentifully in the foothills of the mountains and on high mesas from 5,000 to 8,000 feet elevation. The ashes from the green needles are used to make the juniper ash water. The branches may be gathered anytime of the year.

To Use Water From Juniper Ashes

1   cup hot juniper ashes
2   cups boiling water

Gather juniper branches from trees which have a reddish appearance. Set fire to a handful and hold over a skillet to catch the ashes. Burn only the green needles. To the hot ashes add the boiling water. Stir thoroughly and strain. This water is used as a mordant.

17

RAW ALUM   tsekhǫ'

Raw alum is a low grade, naturally occurring alum. It is found in the form of soft white chunks and is gathered from under rocks in the flat reservation country where there has been recent water evaporation. It is especially plentiful around the sulphur spring deposits in New Mexico.

To Use Raw Alum:

Throw the chunks of alum onto the hot coals until they start to foam. Then drop into the dyebath or if desired add to the dyebath without toasting. The latter method is easier when the dyeing is being done on a stove and is quite satisfactory.

THE DYEING OF YARNS

ACTINEA, SEVERAL-FLOWERED
(ACTINEA LEPTOCLADA)
bee'oołtsoih bee'iiłkhoh

This entire plant is used for dye while in bloom. It grows under the timber in the mountains and reaches a height of about one foot. A number of medium-sized, single-petaled yellow flowers shoots out from the root.

COLOR 1—*Light Greenish Yellow*

2 pounds Actinea leptoclada (blossom and leaves)

¼ cup raw alum

1 pound yarn

Boil blossoms and leaves in 5 gallons of water in a tin or aluminum vessel for two hours. Strain. Add the raw alum to the dyewater. Stir and boil 10 minutes. Add the wet yarn and stir again. Let boil 15 minutes for this tint. Remove immediately from dyebath and rinse.

Note: This dyewater may be used a second time for a lighter tint.

ACTINEA, SINGLE-FLOWERED
(ACTINEA GAILLARDIA)
be'oochidi bee 'iiłkhoh

The flowers, leaves and stems of this plant are used for dye while fresh. It grows about one and one-half feet tall under the timber in the mountains. One yellow blossom is sent up from each root. It blooms in June.

COLOR 2—Yellow

1   pound Actinea gailladia (flowers, stems and leaves)
¼   cup raw alum
1   pound yarn

Boil the flowers, leaves, and stems in 5 gallons of water in an enamel or granite vessel for 2 hours. Strain. Add the raw alum to the dyewater. Stir and let boil 10 minutes. Add wet yarn. Stir well. Boil 2 hours. Leave in dyebath overnight. Rinse.

ALDER   (ALNUS TENUIFOLIA)
g'ish

The bark of the male tree is the part used for the dye. It is peeled from the limbs while fresh, and dried unless used immediately. The bark gives the strongest color if it is taken in the fall.

The tree grows plentifully along streams in the mountains and reaches a height of twelve feet.

COLOR 3—Soft Brown

2   pounds alder bark (from male tree).

1   pound yarn

Soak dried alder bark over-night, then boil for 2 hours in 5 gallons of water. Strain. Add wet yarn and stir well. Boil for 2 hours. Leave in the dyebath overnight if desired. Rinse.

COLOR 4—Tan-Beige

Afterbath dye (from "Alder Bark" above)

¼ cup raw alum

1 pound yarn

After removing the first pound of yarn, add ¼ cup raw alum to the remaining dye water. Stir well. Let boil 10 minutes. Add wet yarn. Stir again. Boil 2 hours. Leave in the dyebath overnight if desired. Rinse.

Alder bark is also used with mountain mahogany root to produce several shades of tan and brown. The recipes for these dyes are given under "Mountain Mahogany."

BEEPLANT, ROCKY MOUNTAIN
(CLEOME SERRULATA)
waa'

Beeplant is highly esteemed by the Navajo people, because it has saved the tribe at times from starvation. It grows about three feet high and its purple blossoms color sections of the mesas of the reservation through July and August. The entire plant before it blossomed was used for the dye given below.

COLOR 5—*Yellow Green*

1 bushel beeplant
1 pound yarn

Boil beeplant in 5 gallons of water until very tender. Mash up the leaves and remove the stalks. Add wet yarn and set in a warm place to ferment for 1 week. Rub the dye into the yarn often. Place yarn in dyebath on the stove and let boil for 1 hour. Remove from the fire and allow to ferment another week in the same dyebath. Rinse.

BITTERBALL (TAGETES MICRANTHA)
bįį yildjaa'ih

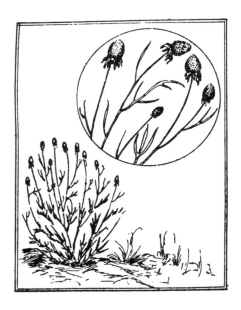

This entire plant while in blossom is used for dye. It grows about two feet high and blooms in early summer. It is a sacred medicine plant, and will probably never be a popular dye plant with the Navajo.

COLOR 6—*Greenish Yellow*

3   pounds bitter ball (entire plant)
½ cup raw alum
1   pound yarn

Boil the leaves and twigs in 6 gallons of water for 1 to 2 hours. Strain. Add the alum. Stir well and boil 10 minutes. Add the wet yarn and stir again. Boil 1 to 3 hours, depending upon the depth of color desired. Allowing it to remain in the dyebath overnight will also deepen and brighten the color. Fewer blossoms will make a lighter shade. Boil in an enamel vessel for this bright yellow color. Rinse.

COLOR 7—Pale Greenish Yellow

Prepare as for "Greenish Yellow" except that the yarn is boiled only ½ hour and removed immediately from the dyebath.

COLOR 8—Mustard

Prepare as for "Greenish Yellow" except that the yarn is dyed in a tin or aluminum vessel.

CACTUS, PRICKLY PEAR
(OPUNTIA POLYCANTHA)
hwoshntxyeedi binesd'ą'

The prickly pear is a low growing cactus, widely distributed on the mesas of New Mexico and Aizona. It has a yellow blossom and a red fruit which ripens the latter part of September. After picking, the fruit must be rubbed in the sand with the foot to remove the spines. It is then used either fresh or sun-dried, but it requires a little more of the dried fruit than of the fresh to give the same color.

COLOR 9—Rose

2   pounds fresh cactus fruit (3 if dried)

1   pound yarn

   Squeeze the juice from the fruit and strain into 3 gallons of cool water. If the fruit has been dried, soak before squeezing. Add wet yarn. Let stand in

a warm place for a week to ferment. Rub the dye into the yarn often. Rinse.

   Note: This dye cannot be boiled. To do so causes it to lose its color and the yarn becomes tan instead. The fermentation must take place in an earthenware or enamel kettle. If done in tin or aluminum, the color is lost.

COLOR 10—Deep Rose

Prepare in the same manner as for "Rose" except that the rose yarn is put into a second dyebath of the same strength as the first and allowed to ferment in it for a second week.

COLOR 11—Light Rose

Afterbath dyewater from the "Rose" recipe given above

1   pound yarn

Add the wet yarn to the afterbath dyewater and proceed in a manner similar to the directions given in the "Rose" recipe.

COLOR 12—Pink With a Tan Tint

2   pounds fresh cactus fruit

1   pound yarn

Boil 1 pound of the cactus fruit in 4 gallons of water for 1 hour and strain. Add wet yarn. Boil 1 to 2 hours. This makes a tan yarn. Now squeeze the juice from the other pound of cactus fruit and strain into 3 gallons lukewarm water. Add the tan yarn. Let stand in a warm place for a week to ferment. Rub the yarn often to work the dye into it. Rinse well.

COLOR 13—Tan

1   pound cactus fruit

1   pound yarn

Boil the cactus fruit in 4 gallons of water for 1 hour and strain. Bring dyewater to a boil. Add wet yarn. Stir well. Boil 1 to 2 hours. Leave in dyebath overnight. Rinse thoroughly.

CACTUS FRUIT AND MOUNTAIN MAHOGANY ROOT BARK
AFTERBATH DYEWATERS

COLOR 14—Coral Pink

1-½ gallons afterbath dyewater (from "Rose" color above)

1-½ gallons afterbath dyewater (from "Mountain Mahogany Root Bark" recipe found under "Mahogany")

¼   pound yarn

Mix afterbath dyewaters together while cold. Do not heat. Add wet yarn. Stir well. Allow to ferment in a warm place for four days or longer if a deeper shade is desired. Rub the yarn often to work the dye into it. Rinse well.

Prickly pear cactus fruit is also used with mountain mahogany root bark to obtain a rose taupe and a soft reddish tan. The recipes for these dyes are given under "Mahogany."

CANYAIGRE   (RUMEX HYMENOSEPALUS)

chaqd'iniih

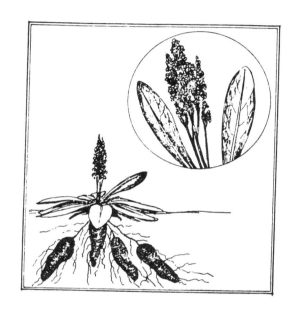

Canyaigre grows on sandy mesas on the reservation. It is a large native dock with leaves which grow about two inches in width, dark green in color and meaty in substance. It has one flower stock arising from the center. The roots of the plant, which are the part used for the dye, resemble sweet potatoes and are very rich in tannic acid. They may be used fresh or after having been split and sundried.

COLOR 15—*Medium Brown*

1   pound dried canyaigre roots
1   pound yarn

Boil canyaigre roots in 4 gallons of water for 1 hour. Mash to liberate the dye substances. Strain. Add wet yarn. Stir well. Boil 1 to 2 hours. Leave in dyebath overnight if a deeper color is desired. Rinse.

COLOR 16—Yellow-Orange

½ pound canyaigre roots
¼ cup raw alum
1 pound yarn

Boil the canyaigre roots in 4 gallons of water for 1 hour. Mash to liberate dye substances. Strain. Add alum. Let boil. Stir well. Add wet yarn. Stir again. Boil 1 to 2 hours. Leave in dyebath overnight if a deeper color is desired.

CELERY, WILD (PSEUDOCYMOPTERUS MONTANUS)

haza'aleehtsoh

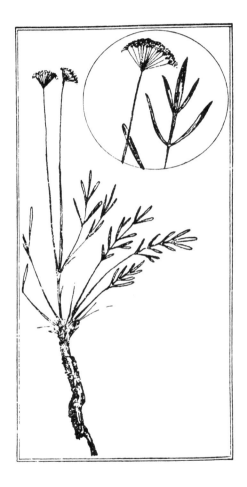

This is a frail-looking plant which is found in the timber regions in the mountains. It grows about one foot high and blooms in June and July. The entire plant is used for dye while fresh.

COLOR 17—Light Canary Yellow

1 pound wild celery (flowers and leaves)
¼ cup raw alum
1 pound yarn

Boil wild celery flowers and leaves in 5 gallons of water in a tin or a-luminum vessel for two hours. Strain. Add the raw alum to the dyewater. Stir and let boil 10 minutes. Add wet yarn and stir well. Let boil 15 minutes. Remove immediately from dyebath and rinse.

Note: This dyewater may be used to color a second pound of yarn a lighter tint.

CHAMIZO   (ATRIPLEX CANESCENS)
diwozhiiłbaih

This shrub is always green and its leaves and twigs may be gathered any time for dye. The blossoms are also used when present on the plant. It grows about three feet high and is common on the mesas throughout New Mexico and Arizona. There are male and female plants of this species and either is suitable.

COLOR 18—*Bright Yellow*

3   pounds chamizo leaves, twigs, and blossoms
½   cup raw alum
1   pound yarn

Boil the blossoms and twigs in 6 gallons of water for 1 to 2 hours. Strain. Add the alum. Stir well and boil 10 minutes. Add the wet yarn and stir again. Boil 1 to 3 hours, depending upon the depth of color desired. Allowing it to remain in the dyebath ovenight will also deepen and brighten the color. Fewer blossoms will make a lighter shade. Boil in an enamel vessel for this bright yellow color. Rinse.

COLOR 19—Light Canary Yellow

Prepare as for "Bright Yellow" except that the yarn is boiled only ½ hour and removed immediately from the dyebath.

COLOR 20—Mustard

Prepare as for the "Bright Yellow" except that the yarn is dyed in a tin or aluminum vessel.

CHOKECHERRY (PRUNUS MELANOCARPA)
didzedig'ozhiih

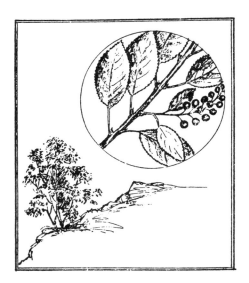

The chokecherry is found in middle elevations in the mountains. It grows about eight to ten feet tall. The bark and roots are suitable for dye purposes.

CHOKECHERRY ROOT BARK AND WILD PLUM ROOT BARK

COLOR 21—*Purplish-Brown*

1   pound chokecherry root bark
1   pound wild plum root bark
1   pound yarn

Break up the bark which has been peeled from the roots. Add 5 gallons water and let soak overnight. Boil for 2 hours. Strain. Add wet yarn to the dye-water and stir well. Boil 2 hours. Let remain in dyebath overnight. Rinse.

CLAW, OWL'S (HELENIUM HOOPESII)
g'asdah bee gąh

This plant is a favorite dye plant with the Navajo. It grows about three feet high. It has long narrow leaves and one yellow blossom on each flower stem. It is found in the meadows in the high mountains and blooms the latter part of June or the first part of July. The entire plant when in blossom is used for dye purposes while fresh.

COLOR 22—*Bright Yellow*

3 pounds owl's claw (leaves, twigs, and blossoms)
½ cup raw alum
1 pound yarn

Boil the blossoms and twigs in 6 gallons of water for 1 to 2 hours. Strain. Add the alum. Stir well and boil 10 minutes. Add the wet yarn and stir again. Boil 1 to 3 hours, depending upon the depth of color desired. Allowing it to remain in the dyebath overnight will also deepen and brighten the color. Fewer blossoms will make a lighter shade. Boil in an enamel vessel for this bright yellow color. Rinse.

COLOR 23—Light Canary Yellow

Prepare as for "Bright Yellow" except that the yarn is boiled only ½ hour and removed immediately from the dyebath.

COLOR 24—Mustard

Prepare as for the "Bright Yellow" except that the yarn is dyed in a tin or aluminum vessel.

GRAPE, OREGON   (BERBERIS AQUIFOLIUM)
chech'il ntł'izi yild'aǫ'ih

The Oregon grape grows commonly in the mountains 8,000 feet altitude and above. The entire plant was used for the dye described below. It may be used fresh or dried.

COLOR 25—*Dulled Greenish Yellow*

4   pounds Oregon grape (roots, leaves and stems)

¼ cup raw alum

1   pound yarn

Boil Oregon grape vines in 5 gallons of water in a granite vessel for 2 hours. Strain. Add the raw alum to the dyewater. Stir and let boil 10 minutes. Add wet yarn. Stir again. Leave in dyebath ovenight. Rinse.

IRONWOOD OR WILD PRIVET
(FORESTIERA NEOMEXICANA)
mǫ'iiadǫ' or g'iishzniniih

The first Navajo name means coyote food. The ironwood tree grows on the foothills of the mountains. The red fruit ripens the latter part of August and turns blue when it is dead ripe. The Navajo use the berries and twigs for ceremonial purposes and for this reason they will not eat them. The very ripe berries are used in making this gray dye.

COLOR 26—*Light Gray*

2   pounds ripe ironwood berries
1   pound yarn
    Boil berries 15 minutes in 4 gallons of water. Strain. Add wet yarn and stir well. Boil ½ hour. Remove from fire and allow to ferment in the dyebath 4 days for this shade. Rinse.

JUNIPER, ONE-SEEDED (JUNIPERUS MONOSPERMA)
gad

This tree has been described under "Mordants."
The bast and twigs and the berries, if desired, may be used for dye.

COLOR 27—*Orange-Tan*

2   pounds juniper bast and twigs
¼   cup raw alum
1   pound yarn
    Boil juniper bast and twigs in 4 gallons of water for 1 hour. Strain. Add alum and let boil. Stir well. Add wet yarn and stir again. Boil 1 to 2 hours, depending upon depth of color desired. Leave in dyewater overnight. Rinse.

COLOR 28—*Yellow-Tan*

    Prepare in the same manner as for "Orange-Tan," but omit the raw alum and use no mordant.

LARKSPUR, WILD PURPLE
(DELPHINIUM SCAPOSUM)
txadidiįdootł'izh

This dainty plant with a purple flower grows in timber on the desert where there is little moisture. It is a sacred plant to the Navajo, its purple petals being used in some of their ceremonies. For this reason many Navajo will not use it for dye. It has been reported that the purple petals yield a purple dye. The experiments at the school have failed to give a color even approaching it either by fermenting the plant or boiling it. The purple petals or the entire plant may be used for dye.

COLOR 29—*Greenish Gray*

2   pounds purple larkspur petals.
1   pound yarn

Pour enough warm water over the petals to cover. Soak a day and then mash them. Add wet yarn and allow to ferment in a warm place for 1 week. Work the dye into the yarn often. Rinse.

COLOR 30—Light Greenish Yellow

2   pounds purple larkspur (flowers, leaves, stems)
¼   cup raw alum
1   pound yarn

Boil larkspur in 5 gallons of water in a granite or enamel vessel for 2 hours. Strain. Add the raw alum to the dyewater. Stir and let boil 10 minutes. Add wet yarn. Stir again. Boil 2 hours. Leave in dyebath overnight. Rinse.

LICHEN, GROUND   (PARMELIA MOLLUSCULA)
nį'hadlaad

These tiny plants cling to the ground under sagebrush and trees on certain mesas in the Southwest. The entire plant is boiled for dye. They may be used fresh or dried.

Stone lichen (tsedlaad may be similarly used.) They grow on stones in the foothills of the mountains in the Southwest and are easily scraped off after a rain loosens them.

COLOR 31—*Light Orange*

1   pound ground lichens
¼ cup raw alum
1   pound yarn

Boil lichens in 4 gallons of water for 1 hour. Strain. Add alum and let boil. Stir well. Add wet yarn and stir again. Boil ½ hour. Rinse.

COLOR 32—Reddish-Tan

½ pound ground lichens
¼ cup raw alum
1 pound yarn

Boil lichens in 4 gallons of water for 1 hour. Strain. Add alum and let boil. Stir well. Add wet yarn and stir again. Boil 1 to 2 hours, depending upon depth of color desired. Less alum and a shorter boiling time produces a lighter color. Leaving it in the dyebath overnight gives a deeper shade. Rinse.

COLOR 33—Yellow-Tan

Prepare as for "Reddish-Tan" except that the water from 1 cup juniper ashes is used instead of raw alum as a mordant.

Gound lichens may be used with mountain mahogany root to produce light red-brown. The recipe for this dye is given under "Mahogany."

LUPINE, BLUE-FLOWERED   (LUPINUS KINGII)

'azee' diilch'iłiih or łi͡i'daǫ'

Lupines grow quite commonly in the mountains and reach a height of one and one-half to two feet. They begin to bloom in June and the entire plants are used while fresh.

COLOR 34—Greenish Yellow

4   pounds lupine (flowers, leaves, stems)
¼   cup raw alum
1   pound yarn

Boil the flowers, leaves and stems in 5 gallons of water in an enamel or granite vessel for 2 hours. Strain. Add the raw alum to the dyewater. Stir and let boil 10 minutes. Add wet yarn. Stir well. Boil 2 hours. Leave in dyebath overnight. Rinse.

MAHOGANY, MOUNTAIN
(CERCOCARPUS MONTANUS)
tse 'esdaaziih

The bark of the root of this tree is red and is the part used for dye. It gives the strongest color when dug in the fall.

The tree which grows four to eight feet in height is found commonly in the mountains and on the foothills at an elevation of 7,000 to 10,000 feet.

MOUNTAIN MAHOGANY ROOT BARK

COLOR 35—Soft, Reddish-Brown

2   pounds mountain mahogany root bark
1   pound yarn

Boil mountain mahogany root bark for 2 hours in 5 gallons of water. Strain. Add wet yarn and boil for 2 hours. Stir well. Leave in dyebath overnight. Rinse thoroughly.

MOUNTAIN MAHOGANY ROOT BARK (WITH JUNIPER ASHES)

COLOR 36—Deep Reddish-Brown

2   pounds mountain mahograny root bark
Water from 1 cup juniper ashes
1   pound yarn

Boil mountain mahogany root bark in 5 gallons of water for 2 hours. Strain. Add juniper ash water to the dyebath. (The method of preparation is described under "Mordants.") Stir and boil 15 minutes. Add wet yarn and stir well. Boil 1 hour and leave in the dyebath overnight. Rinse thoroughly.

MOUNTAIN MAHOGANY ROOT BARK AND CACTUS FRUIT NO. 1

COLOR 37—Rose Taupe

1   pound mountain mahogany root bark
1   pound dried prickly pear cactus fruit
Water from one cup juniper ashes
1   pound yarn

Boil the mountain mahogany for an hour in 5 gallons of water. Strain. Cool until lukewarm. Soak the cactus fruit in 1 quart of water overnight and strain, squeezing the pulp through. Combine with the mountain mahogany solution. Add the wet yarn, which has been soaked for a few minutes in the juniper ash water. Allow to ferment in a warm place for one week. Rub the dye into the yarn often. Rinse thoroughly.

MOUNTAIN MAHOGANY ROOT BARK AND CACTUS FRUIT NO. 2

COLOR 38—Soft, Reddish-Tan

1   pound mountain mahogany root bark
1   pound dried prickly pear cactus fruit
1   pound yarn

Boil the mountain mahogany root bark for an hour in 5 gallons of water. Strain and cool until lukewarm. Soak the cactus fruit in 1 quart of water and strain, squeezing the pulp through. Combine with the mountain mahogany solution. Add wet yarn and allow to ferment in a warm place for one week. Rub the dye into the yarn often. Rinse thoroughly.

This makes a beautiful background color.

The afterbath dyewater from mountain mahogany root bark and prickly pear cactus fruit may be used to obtain a coral pink. The recipe for this dye is given under "Cactus Fruit."

Fresh cactus fruit may be used. The same amount will give a slightly deeper color, or slightly less may be used.

MOUNTAIN MAHOGANY ROOT BARK AND NAVAJO TEA NO. 1

COLOR 39—*Dark Burnt Orange*

1 pound mountain mahogany root bark
2 pounds Navajo tea
½ cup raw alum
1 pound yarn

Soak mountain mahogany root bark and Navajo tea overnight in 5 gallons of water. Boil 1 hour and strain. Bring dyewater to a boil and add alum. Stir well and let boil 10 minutes. Add wet yarn and stir again. Boil 2 hours and remove immediately from the dyebath. Rinse well.

MOUNTAIN MAHOGANY ROOT BARK AND NAVAJO NO. 2

COLOR 40—*Henna*

Prepare as for "Mountain Mahogany Root Bark and Navajo Tea No. 1" except that instead of removing the yarn from the dyebath immediately after boiling, allow it to ferment in the dyewater for 1 week. Rub the dye into the yarn often. Rinse.

MOUNTAIN MAHOGANY ROOT BARK AND GROUND LICHENS

COLOR 41—*Light Red-Brown*

1 pound mountain mahogany root bark
½ pound ground lichens
Water from 1 cup juniper ashes
1 pound yarn

Boil the bark and the lichens together in 5 gallons of water for 2 hours. Strain. Add juniper ash water. (The method of preparing juniper ash water is described under "Mordants".) Stir well. Boil 15 minutes. Add wet yarn and stir again. Boil 2 hours. Leave in the dyebath overnight. Rinse.

MOUNTAIN MAHOGANY ROOT BARK AND ALDER BARK NO. 1

COLOR 42—*Light Brown*

1 pound mountain mahogany root bark
1 pound alder bark
¼ cup raw alum
1 pound yarn

Soak mountain mahogany root bark and alder bark in 5 gallons of water overnight. Boil 1 hour and strain. Then add raw alum and boil 10 minutes, stirring constantly. Add wet yarn. Stir well. Boil 2 hours. Leave in dyebath overnight. Rinse thoroughly.

MOUNTAIN MAHOGANY ROOT BARK AND ALDER BARK NO. 2

COLOR 43—Reddish-Tan

2 pounds mountain mahogany root bark
½ pound alder bark
1 pound yarn

Soak the two barks in 5 gallons of water overnight. Then boil 1 hour and strain. Bring to a boil and add wet yarn. Stir well. Boil 1 hour and remove from dyebath immediately. Rinse thoroughly.

MOUNTAIN MAHOGANY ROOT BARK AND ALDER BARK NO. 3

COLOR 44—Soft, Cream Tan

2 pounds mountain mahogany root bark
½ pound alder bark
1 pound yarn

Soak the barks in 3 gallons of warm water for 1 to 2 days (the color of many plant materials, especially if dried, seems to come out into the water better if they are allowed to ferment a little before being strained out). Strain. Add wet yarn. Let stand in a warm place for a week to ferment. Rub the dye into the yarn often. Rinse well.

MOUNTAIN MAHOGANY ROOT BARK AND ALDER BARK NO. 4

COLOR 45—Light Brown

1 pound mountain mahogany root bark
1 cup juniper ashes
½ pound alder bark
1 pound yarn

Boil mountain mahogany and alder barks in 6 gallons of water for 1 hour. Strain. Add water from juniper ashes. (Method of preparation is described under 'Mordants".) Boil 15 minutes. Wet the yarn and add to the dyebath. Stir well. Let boil 2 hours. Rinse thoroughly.

OAK, GAMBEL'S   (QUERCUS GAMBELII)
chech'l bikhashd'oozh

The bark of this tree is the part used for the dye and gives the strongest color when gathered in the fall. It is stripped from the wood immediately and may be used either fresh or dried. Gambel's oak grows commonnly in the lower mountains.

GAMBEL'S OAK BARK

COLOR 46—Dulled Tan

8   pounds Gambels' oak bark
½ cup raw alum
1   pound yarn

Pound up the bark and boil in 5 gallons of water for 2 hours. Strain. Add the raw alum to the dyewater and boil 10 minutes. Add the wet yarn and stir again. Boil for 2 hours. Allow to remain in the dyebath overnight. Rinse.

OAK, SCRUB (QUERCUS PUNGENS)
chech'ilntł'izih

The scrub tree is found in the low mountains. The gall which grows on it is the part used for dye.

GALL FROM SCRUB OAK

COLOR 47—Light Gold

4   pounds gall (green or brown)
¼   cup raw alum
1   pound yarn

Pulverize the gall and boil in 5 gallons of water for 2 hours. Strain. Add the raw alum to the dyewater and boil 10 minutes. Place the wet yarn into the dyebath and stir well. Boil for 2 hours. Allow to remain in the dyewater overnight. Rinse.

1   pound gall (brown or green)

COLOR 48—Light Yellowish-Tan

¼ cup raw alum

1   pound yarn

Pulverize the gall and boil in 5 gallons of water for 2 hours. Strain. Add raw alum to the dyewater. Stir and boil 10 minutes. Place the wet yarn in the dyebath and stir well. Boil for two hours. Allow to remain in the dyebath overnight. Rinse.

PAINTBRUSH, INDIAN   (CASTILLEJA INTEGRE)

dahitxįhidaq'

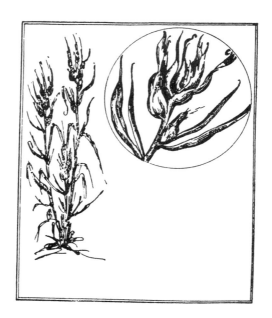

The Navajo name means hummingbird food. It grows one to one and one-half feet tall and is found in the lower parts of the mountains. Either the flowers alone or the entire plant may be used for dye purposes. It blossoms in June and July and is used while fresh.

INDIAN PAINTBRUSH BLOSSOMS

COLOR 49—*Tan*

4 pounds Indian paintbrush blossoms
Cold water to cover
1 pound yarn

Pour enough cold water over the blossoms to cover. Soak a day or two and mash up the blossoms. Remove hard stems. Add wet yarn to dyebath and allow to ferment in a warm place for 1 week. Work the dye into the yarn often. Rinse.

INDIAN PAINTBRUSH (ENTIRE PLANT)

COLOR 50—Greenish Yellow

2   pounds Indian paintbrush (stems, leaves, and blossoms)
¼   cup raw alum
1   pound yarn

Boil Indian paintbrush in 5 gallons of water in an enamel or granite vessel for 2 hours. Strain. Add the raw alum to the dyewater. Stir and let boil 10 minutes. Add wet yarn and stir again. Boil 2 hours. Leave in dyewater overnight. Rinse.

PINEDROP   (PTEROSPORA ANDROMEDEA)

ndoochii'

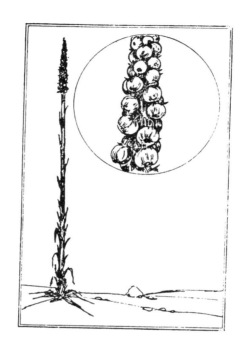

This plant which is found in the open woods presents an unusual appearance. It grows about two feet high, has a reddish-brown stalk with round, drop-like, brown berries shooting out on all sides on the upper part of the stalk. It is gathered in the late summer or early fall and may be used either fresh or dried. The entire plant is made into the dye.

COLOR 51—Dull Tan

1   pound dry pinedrop (entire plant)
¼   cup raw alum
1   pound yarn

Pulverize the plant and boil in 5 gallons of water for 2 hours. Strain. Add the raw alum to the dyewater. Stir and boil 10 minutes. Place the wet yarn in the dyebath and stir again. Boil for 2 hours. Allow to remain in the dyebath overnight. Rinse.

PLUM, WILD   (PRUNUS AMERICANA)
didzeh

The wild plum is not common on the reservation but has been introduced in some places. The tree grows five to eight feet high. The roots give the purple dye.

WILD PLUM ROOTS

COLOR 52—Reddish-Purple

2   pounds wild plum roots
¼ cup raw alum
1   pound yarn

Boil the roots in 6 gallons of water for 1 to 2 hours. Strain. Add the alum. Stir well and boil 10 minutes. Add the wet yarn and stir again. Boil 1 to 3 hours, depending upon the depth of color desired. Leave in dyebath overnight. Rinse.

RABBITBRUSH, BIG
(CHRYSOTHAMNUS LATISQUAMEUS)
g'iiłtsoih

The shrub is found very commonly in arroyos or places where a little water is available. It grows four or five feet in height and is covered with fluffy, yellow blossoms in the late summer and early fall. The flowers and twigs while fresh are used for dye.

COLOR 53—*Bright Yellow*

3 pounds rabbitbrush blossoms and twigs
½ cup raw alum
1 pound yarn

Boil the blossoms and twigs in 6 gallons of water for 1 to 2 hours. Strain. Add the alum. Stir well and boil 10 minutes. Add the wet yarn and stir again. Boil 1 to 3 hours, depending upon the depth of color desired. Allowing it to remain in the dyebath overnight will also deepen and brighten the color. Fewer blossoms will make a lighter shade. Boil in an enamel vessel for this bright yellow color. Rinse.

56

COLOR 54—*Light Canary Yellow*

Prepare as for "Bright Yellow" except that the yarn is boiled only $\frac{1}{2}$ hour and removed immediately from the dyebath.

COLOR 55—*Mustard*

Prepare as for the "Bright Yellow" except that the yarn is dyed in a tin or aluminum vessel.

RABBITBRUSH, SMALL
(CHRYSOTHAMNUS BIGELOVII)
g'iiłtsoididjoolih

This species of rabbitbrush is found out on the flat open mesas but is not very common. It grows about two feet high and blooms during the late summer and early fall. The twigs and blossoms are used for dye.

COLOR 56—Bright Yellow

3   pounds rabbitbrush blossoms and twigs
½   cup raw alum
1   pound yarn

Boil the blossoms and twigs in 6 gallons of water for 1 to 2 hours. Strain. Add the alum. Stir well and boil 10 minutes. Add the wet yarn and stir again. Boil 1 to 3 hours, depending upon the depth of color desired. Allowing it to remain in the dyebath overnight will also deepen and brighten the color. Fewer blossoms will make a lighter shade. Boil in an enamel vessel for this bright yellow color. Rinse.

COLOR 57—*Light Canary Yellow*

Prepare as for "Bright Yellow" except that the yarn is boiled only ½ hour and removed immediately from the dyebath.

COLOR 58—*Mustard*

Prepare as for the "Bright Yellow" except that the yarn is dyed in a tin or aluminum vessel.

ROSE, CLIFF (COWANIA STANSBURIANA)

'awee'ds'aal

Cliff rose is a signal plant to the Navajo. If it blooms late in October, it is believed to indicate that there will be deep snow during the winter. Its little white blossoms appear in the early summer. Its evergreen twigs may be used for dye at any season of the year. It grows commonly on the lower parts of the mountains.

COLOR 59—*Gold*

2   pounds fresh cliff rose (twigs and leaves)
¼ cup raw alum
1   pound yarn

Boil the twigs and leaves in 5 gallons of water for 2 hours. Strain. Add raw alum to the dyewater. Stir and let boil 10 minutes. Add the wet yarn and stir again. Boil for 2 hours. Allow to remain in the dyebath overnight. Rinse.

RUBBERPLANT   (HYMENOXYS METCALFEI)
ne'eshdjaa' yilkhyee'eh

The Navajo name means resembling eared owl's foot. This plant which blooms in July and August grows to be about one foot high. It is very common in the timber regions on the mountains. It is a rubber plant, although not the Colorado rubber plant which is so common throughout New Mexico. The leaves, stems, and yellow flowers are used for dye and may be either fresh or dried.

COLOR 60—*Bright Yellow*

3   pounds rubberplant (leaves, stems, and flowers)
½ cup raw alum
1   pound yarn

Boil the blossoms and twigs in 6 gallons of water for 1 to 2 hours. Strain. Add the alum. Stir well and boil 10 minutes. Add the wet yarn and stir again. Boil 1 to 3 hours, depending upon the depth of color desired. Allowing it to remain in the dyebath overnight will also deepen and brighten the color. Fewer blossoms will make a lighter shade. Boil in an enamel vessel for this bright yellow color. Rinse.

COLOR 61—*Light Canary Yellow*

Prepare as for "Bright Yellow" except that the yarn is boiled only ½ hour and removed immediately from the dyebath.

COLOR 62—*Mustard*

Prepare as for the "Bright Yellow" except that the yarn is dyed in a tin or aluminum vessel.

SAGEBRUSH, BASIN   (ARTEMISA TRIDENTATA)

ds'ah

This shrub grows three and four feet high. It is one of the most charac-teristic plants between 4,500 and 8,000 feet altitude in northern and north-western New Mexico. The Navajo consider it a very valuable plant, because it is used for medicine and forage as well as for dye. It is always green and its leaves and twigs may be used the year round.

COLOR 63—*Slight Greenish Yellow*

3   pounds sagebrush leaves and twigs
½ cup raw alum
1   pound yarn

Boil the leaves and twigs in 6 gallons of water for 1 to 2 hours. Strain. Add the alum. Stir well and boil 10 minutes. Add the wet yarn and stir again. Boil 1 to 3 hours, depending upon the depth of color desired. Allowing it to re-main in the dyebath overnight will also deepen and brighten the color. Fewer twigs will make a lighter shade. Boil in an enamel vessel for this bright yellow color. Rinse.

COLOR 64—*Pale Greenish Yellow*

Prepare as for "Slight Greenish Yellow" except that the yarn is boiled only ½ hour and removed immediately from the dyebath.

COLOR 65—*Mustard*

Prepare as for "Slight Greenish Yellow" except that the yarn is dyed in a tin or aluminum vessel.

COLOR 66—*Gold*

3   pounds sagebrush
½   cup raw alum
1   pound yarn

Boil the twigs and leaves in 5 gallons of water for 2 hours. Strain. Add raw alum to the dyewater. Stir and let boil 10 minutes. Add the wet yarn and stir again. Boil gently about 6 hours. Allow to remain in dyewater overnight. Rinse.

COLOR 67—*Rich Olive Green*

2   pounds sagebrush
1   cup raw alum
Afterbath black dyewater (from recipe given under "Sumac, Piñon, and Yellow Ocher.")
13 pound yarn

Dye the yarn yellow first with sage and alum described above for "Slight Greenish Yellow." Remove from dyebath and add to the boiling afterbath black dyewater. Let boil two hours. Leave in dyebath overnight. Rinse.

COLOR 68—*Medium Olive Green*

4   pounds sagebrush
1   cup raw alum
Afterbath black dyewater (from recipe given under Sumac, Piñon, and Yellow Ocher.")
1   pound yarn

The method of preparation is the same as for "Rich Olive Green" above.

SUMAC, THREE-LEAVED   (RHUS TRILOBATA)
chiiłchin or g'ił',

PITCH OF THE PIÑON   (PINUS EDULIS)
cha'oł bidjeeh,

AND YELLOW OCHER
łeetsoh

SUMAC

Sumac withes with leaves, piñon pitch and yellow ocher, a mineral, are used in making black dye.

Sumac is also called squaw bush and skunk bush. It is a shrub which grows three to six feet high, depending upon the amount of moisture. It grows where ever a little water is available, as along arroyos and streams. The withes with leaves are used for making black dye and may be either fresh or dried. fourth pound each.

The piñon is found on the foothills of the mountains of New Mexico and Arizona at an elevation of 4,000 to 8,000 feet. It is an evergreen tree which grows ten feet and higher, depending upon the amount of moisture. The pitch which oozes out of the tree and collects on the bark is used for this dye.

The mineral, yellow ocher, is a type of gypsum with a little iron in it. It may be picked up around coal mines in the arid regions on the Navajo Reservation. It is found in soft, yellow chunks.

COLOR 69—*Bluish Black* (generally known as the native black dye)

2   pounds sumac withes with leaves
3   cups piñon pitch
3   cups yellow ocher
1   pound yarn

Roll the sumac in rolls (4 large rolls). In winter use dried leaves only. Boil the sumac with 6 gallons of water from 1 to 3 hours (longer boiling produces a faster color).

Toast the ocher to cocoa brown in a frying pan. Drop in the pitch, a little at a time, stir well as long as it smokes. It should now be shiny like gun powder and a bluish color. Cool the ocher until just warm before using. Caution: This is inflammable, so keep away from flames.

Strain the sumac, add the ocher and pitch, stir and boil 15 minutes. Add wet yarn. Boil 2 to 3 hours. Leave yarn in dyewater overnight. Rinse two or three times and dry. Shake or rub in a cloth to remove loose powder.

Note: If any ocher and pitch mixture is left over, warm a little before using it again.

COLOR 70—Light Oxford Gray

Afterbath native black dyewater from above recipe
1 pound yarn

Add sufficient water to the afterbath black dyewater to make 4 gallons. Bring to a boil. Add wet yarn. Stir well. Boil 2 to 3 hours stirring frequently. For a darker color, allow the yarn to remain in the dyebath overnight. Rinse thoroughly.

SUMAC BERRIES

COLOR 71—Light Orange-Brown

4 pounds ripe sumac berries (dried)
1 pound yarn

Grind sumac berries between Navajo grinding stones. Soak in 3 gallons of lukewarm water for two days or until sufficient fermentation has taken place so that the color of the fruit has passed out into the dyewater. Strain, squeezing the pulp through. Add wet yarn. Let stand in a warm place to ferment. Rub the yarn often to work the dye into it. Rinse well.

TEA, MORMON   (EPHEDRA VIRIDIS)
dɫ'oh'azihih

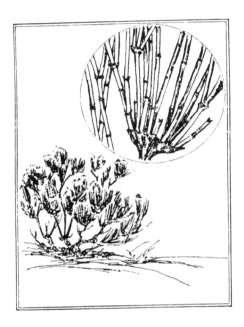

This evergreen shrub grows commonly on the mesas. The twigs with their leaves are used for dye and may be gathered at any time.

COLOR 72—*Light Tan*

2   pounds Mormon tea (twigs and leaves)

¼ cup raw alum

1   pound yarn

Pound the stalks to break them up. Cover with 5 gallons of water and boil 2 hours. Strain. Add raw alum to the dyewater. Stir and boil 10 minutes. Place the wet yarn in the dyebath and stir again. Boil 2 hours. Allow to remain in the dyebath overnight. Rinse.

TEA, NAVAJO (THELESPERMA GRACILE)
ch'ilgohwehih

Navajo tea is common in the timber regions on the mountain and around the edges of cultivated land at high elevations if the moisture is sufficient. It grows from one to two feet tall and its orange blossoms appear in July. The leaves, stems, and flowers are used for dye purposes and may be either fresh or dried. The Navajo twist the stems into small uniform-sized rolls before drying.

COLOR 73—*Orange*

2   pounds dried Navajo tea
½ cup raw alum
1   pound yarn

Boil tea in 5 gallons of water for 1 hour. Strain. Add alum. Let boil. Stir well. Add wet yarn. Stir again. Boil 2 hours and remove immediately from dyebath for this tone of color. Rinse well.

COLOR 74—Light Orange

Afterbath dyewater from the Navajo tea in the above recipe

¼ cup raw alum

1 pound yarn

yarn. Stir again. Boil 2 hours and leave in the dyebath overnight. Rinse tho - oughly.

COLOR 75—Light Olive Green

2 pounds fresh Navajo tea (must be fresh for this color)

1 pound yarn

well. Boil 1 hour. Remove immediately from dyebath. Rinse well.

NAVAJO TEA AND CANYAIGRE ROOT

½ pound fresh Navajo tea

Boil tea in 4 gallons of water for 1 hour and strain. Add wet yarn. Stir

COLOR 76—Orange

Bring afterbath dyewater to a boil and add raw alum. Stir well. Add wet

½ pound dried canyaigre root

½ cup raw alum

1 pound yarn

Soak canyiagre root overnight in 5 gallons of water. Then add Navajo tea and boil 1 hour. Strain. Add alum and boil 10 minutes. Stir well. Add wet yarn. Stir again. Boil 1 hour and remove immediately from dyebath. Rinse well.

Navajo tea is also used with mountain mahogany root bark to obtain a dark burnt orange and a henna. The recipes for these dyes are given under "Mahogany."

NAVAJO TEA AND AFTERBATH BLACK DYEWATER

COLOR 77—Pineneedle Green

2 pounds Navajo tea

½ cup raw alum

Afterbath black dyewater (from recipe given under "Sumac.")

1 pound yarn

Dye the yarn orange first with the Navajo tea and alum as described a- bove for "Orange." Remove from the dyebath and add to the boiling after- bath black dyewater. Stir well. Let boil 2 hours. Leave in dyebath overnight. Rinse thoroughly.

THISTLE, RUSSIAN   (SALSOLA PESTIFER)

ch'ildeeninih

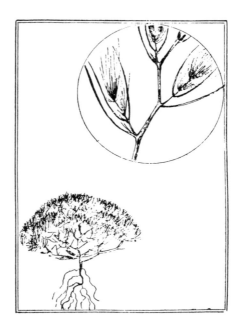

This very troublesome prickly weed grows anywhere at lower altitudes. The entire plant, while young, is used in the recipe given below.

COLOR 78—Dull Olive Green

1   bushel Russian thistle (entire plant)
1   pound yarn

Boil the thistle in 5 gallons of water until very tender. Pull out the stalks. Add wet yarn. Allow leaves to ferment in the dyebath with the yarn for 1 week. Rub the dye into the yarn often. Place yarn in dyebath on the stove and let boil 1 hour. Remove from fire and allow to ferment another week in some dye-water. Rinse twice or until water comes out clear.

COLOR 79—Deep Tan

½ bushel Russian thistle (young plants)
1   pound yarn

Boil thistle in 5 gallons of water until very tender. Pull out the stalks. Add wet yarn. Allow leaves to ferment in dyebath with yarn for one week. Rub the dye into the yarn often. Place yarn in dyebath on the stove and let boil 1 hour. Remove from fire and allow to ferment another week in the same dyewater. Rinse.

WALNUT, WILD   (JUGLANS MAJOR)
ha'a{tsedih

The wild walnut tree is found growing in canyons in New Mexico and Arizona. It grows five and six feet and higher where there is more moisture. The leaves, hulls, and the whole nut are used for dye purposes and may either be fresh or dried.

WILD WALNUT HULLS

COLOR 80—Rich Brown

2   pounds wild walnut hulls

½ cup raw alum

1   pound yarn

Crush the hulls, add 4 gallons of water and let soak overnight. Boil 1 hour longer and strain. Add alum and boil 10 minutes. Stir well. Wet the yarn and place in the dyebath. Stir and let boil 2 hours. Leave in dyebath overnight. Rinse.

Almost any shade of brown can be made by varying the weight of the hulls used. The entire nut may be used if desired.

Note: If the alum is omitted in the above recipe, the color of the yarn is not as deep nor as rich as when alum is used but tends to be a little more gray in color. This shade of brown blends very nicely with bright colors when used as a background.

COLOR 81—Gray-Tan

Afterbath dye water (from "Wild Walnut Hulls" above)

¼ cup raw alum

1 pound yarn

After removing the first pound of yarn, add the raw alum to the remaining dyewater. Stir well. Let boil 10 minutes. Add wet yarn. Stir again. Boil 2 hours. Leave in the dyebath overnight. Rinse.

WILD WALNUTS AND HULLS

COLOR 82—Rich Tan

1 pound whole walnuts and hulls

¼ cup raw alum

1 pound yarn

Add 4 gallons of water to the hulls and whole walnuts. Soak overnight. Then boil 1 hour. Strain. Add alum and boil 10 minutes. Stir well. Wet the yarn and place in the dyebath. Stir and let boil 1 hour. Remove immediately from the dyebath. Rinse thoroughly.

Note: Break the nuts in pieces if a darker shade is desired.

WILD WALNUT LEAVES

COLOR 83—Light Tan

2 pounds wild walnut leaves

¼ cup raw alum

1 pound yarn

Boil the walnut leaves in 4 gallons of water for 1 or 2 hours. Strain. Add alum. Stir well and boil 10 minutes. Add the wet yarn and stir well. Boil 1 to 3 hours, depending upon depth of color desired. Rinse.

THICK BRICK-COLORED RAIN WATER FROM RED MESAS IN NEW MEXICO AND ARIZONA

txohłitchīi'

COLOR 84—Salmon-Pink

4 gallons very thick brick-colored rain water from red mesas in New Mexico and Arizona.

½ pound yarn

Dip up the water which collects in puddles immediately following a heavy rain. Add wet yarn. Stir well. Boil 4 hours, adding clear water to the dyebath as needed to keep sufficient liquid in the pot. Rinse.

The redder the clay used, the deeper will be the color of the yarn.

RED DYE FOR MOCCASINS

Inseparably connected in the minds of the Indians with the dyeing of wool is the dyeing of buckskin ('abanih) for use as moccasins. A mordant and dye materials are also employed in the coloring of buckskin.

Juniper ashes

Mountain mahogany root bark

Alder bark

Tanned deer skin

Pick some branches of juniper and burn them to ashes and rub these ashes into the hair side of tanned deer skin, the hair having been previously removed in the process of tanning.

Boil the roots of the mountain mahogany ('esdoazih), and while still lukewarm, sop the liquid on the ash covered buckskin. Sprinkle dry ground alder bark powder prepared on a metate or Navajo grinding stone all over the surface of the buckskin which has been wet with the mountain mahogany root dye. Fold the buckskin and allow to remain overnight so that the dye will bite in. In the morning the surface of the buckskin will be a red color.

Only one side of the buckskin is dyed, this side being on the outside or hair side. It may be redyed from time to time as desired. The inside of the moccasins is undyed.

*Names indicated this way are in the posession of the publisher. All items are found and identified on two framed sources.

Every effort has been made to be accurate. Checking sources becomes very confusing with conflicting data. DOCK, SORREL and CANAIGRE are three examples, as follows: DOCK: *Oxalia digyna*. SORREL: *Rumex acetasa*. CANAIGRE: *Rumex hymenosepalus*. Some references show these three are the same. Other references give various identification in the same genus or species.

Printed with permission from the
Museum of Northern Arizona
Flagstaff, Arizona, USA

HOPI DYES

mary~russell ferrell colton

foreword by marsha gallagher

Museum of Northern Arizona Press • Flagstaff

Table of Contents

Foreword

THIS NEW ISSUE of Mary-Russell Ferrell Colton's book on Hopi dyes comes at an opportune time. Interest in the use of natural dyes of all kinds has been growing steadily, and amateur and professional craftsmen alike are sure to welcome having this major resource readily available again. The publication also coincides with the fiftieth anniversary of the Museum of Northern Arizona and is a fitting tribute to Mrs. Colton, who, with her husband, was a cofounder of this institution.

An artist herself, Mrs. Colton guided the art interests of the Museum for many years. She planned new exhibits, acquired objects for the collections, and devoted much time and energy to various research and education projects. One of these projects was her detailed study of Hopi dyes. She spent many years discussing dyeing techniques with Hopi artisans, collecting native dyestuffs, and running laboratory experiments to determine proper "recipes." The result was a clearly written compendium of information on Hopi dyes, first published in 1965.

This new issue retains the text and format of the original, which was meant to be a permanent record of Hopi knowledge and was written as a handbook for use by future Hopi dyers. There have, however, been three additions to the 1965 edition: a new cover, a set of color plates, and a list of additional suggested readings. The photographs have been included to show the variety of naturally produced hues that have been and still are being used by Hopi craftsmen to color their textiles and especially their basketry. The suggested readings should be helpful to those who want to learn more about dyeing with natural materials.

Some home dyers may find it difficult or impractical to exactly duplicate the ingredients and procedures outlined in *Hopi Dyes*. While reasonable cautions should be employed (some mordants and plants are poisonous), a dyer's own experience will allow for experimentation and substitution. For example, as a mordant, commercial alum (potassium aluminum sulfate) could be substituted for the native type, but the quantity used would vary. In some instances household ammonia might be used in place of urine in the dying process, as in a final rinse or bath; in other cases, such as indigo dyeing, ammonia would not be an advisable substitute. As for dyestuffs, related plant species or varieties can sometimes be used interchangeably. The results may approach those of the Hopi dyes. One experiment with a commercial red corn yielded a hue similar to that produced by *koko' ma*, but a substitution of commercial sunflower seeds for the native variety was not nearly so successful. However, in vegetable dyeing no two dyebaths, even those using the same recipe, are ever exactly alike. Variation in color is part of the challenge and fascination of working with natural materials. In fact, this is one of the principal pleasures in working from a book like *Hopi Dyes*.

1978   Marsha Gallagher

                                        Registrar of Anthropology
                                        Museum of Northern Arizona

Introduction

THE WORK DESCRIBED in this paper has covered many years, mostly between 1930 and 1945, first in the field and then in the laboratory.

It is written primarily for the Hopi themselves and especially for the "young people" who, in a rapidly changing world, tend to forget the accomplishments and discoveries of their own people.

The "recipes" presented in this paper have all been tested by the writer and assembled in a workable form. The materials used and their treatment in the laboratory follow primitive procedure as closely as possible. These procedures are "time consuming" and as "time" today is extremely valuable, the Hopi dyer need have no fear that his art will ever be commercialized.

The writer is a painter and technician, a graduate of the Philadelphia School of Design for Women, now called the Moore Institute of Art and Industry. She served as Curator of Art at the Museum of Northern Arizona from 1928 to 1952. From 1952 to 1963 she was Chairman of the Arts Committee of the Board of Trustees of the Northern Arizona Society of Science and Art, Inc., which operates the Museum.

At the Museum, special emphasis was placed on the maintenance and encouragement of Indian Art. The first "Hopi Craftsman" exhibition was held in July, 1930. These annual exhibitions still continue and are held each year at the same time.

The background work in the field for the exhibitions was of special importance and has yielded information not previously recorded.

Every year many trips were made to the Hopi villages where

we lived in the homes of the people or camped nearby. When the Hopi understood what we wished to do, they taught us many things and insisted that we learn the correct procedures. Many of the processes described here have, in the past, been regarded as the property of certain clans, families or individuals and are practiced in a secret manner. Thus, with the death of an individual or passing of a clan, much knowledge was lost, and remained with the people, only as a vague rumor.

The writer gratefully wishes to acknowledge the understanding cooperation of the Hopi craftsmen, men and women, old and young. They have enabled us to record their knowledge and use of vegetable dyes, minerals, and stains permanently for them in this book.

The dye plants were identified by Mr. A. F. Whiting and published by the Museum of Northern Arizona, Bull. 15, 1939.

CHAPTER I

Prehistoric Dyes

THE PREHISTORIC PUEBLOAN PEOPLES of the Southwest were master craftsmen. Expert weavers and dyers, basket makers and potters, their arts were varied, colorful and thriving, when History first discovered them in New Mexico and Arizona.

From the earliest Spanish records to the American invasion, old documents abound in references to the arts of these peoples, whom the Conquistadors marveled to find living in cities and practicing the "civilized arts."*

As the Spaniards themselves were no mean artisans, we may judge that the arts of the Puebloans were highly developed and enjoying a period of "Renaissance." "Embroidered and painted cotton textiles" are frequently mentioned, and also the quality and abundance of the large ollas and beautiful painted bowls.

The prehistory of the "Cultural Ancestors" of these people, is slowly revealing the early pueblo dweller and his fore-runner, the "Basketmaker," as artisans of remarkable skill and invention, to whom the craftsman of today cannot compare, for in most cases he cherishes only vague memories of past skills.

In the Basketmaker period, 500 to 700 A.D., the ancestors of the Hopi, not yet possessing cotton, skilfully wove and dyed yucca and other vegetable fibers, fashioning these harsh materials into clothing, sandals, matting and baskets of great beauty.

Then came cotton, the most precious of all vegetable fibers in the New World. At first, it must have been scarce, for we see it used sparingly, combined with coarser fibers. Finally it appears alone, as the main textile fiber of the prehistoric Puebloan while

* Kent, 1957, pp. 478-483, 487.

the other vegetable fibers take their place for basketry, sandals, matting, etc.

With the coming of a white fiber like cotton, the dyer's art must have received a great impetus, for it made possible the use of an infinite number of shades not effective upon the darker fibers.

This was apparently the case, for spun cotton textiles embellished with designs in shades of rust, red, orange, yellow, brown, black, dull blues and purples have been recorded from excavated material.

These conditions apparently continued to flourish up to the advent of the Spaniard.

There was definitely no wide-spread decadence in the arts from the Basketmaker to the historic period, but rather a steady progression toward a general "Renaissance" of Puebloan arts.

With the coming of a new race, there also arrived a strange new animal, the sheep, whose advent completely changed the textile industries of the Puebloan and stimulated the nomadic Navajo to adopt the arts of their sedentary neighbors. When the Pueblo people acquired sheep from their Spanish conquerors and found that the long white fibers of wool could be spun and woven into excellent cloth and with far less exertion than required for cotton, the next step was naturally the decoration by coloring of these new fibers.

Therefore, it is reasonable to suppose that a Hopi, upon receiving new material which he wanted to dye, would first try upon this material, the dyes and mordants with which he was familiar in the dying of cotton. We may find in use today only those dyes which could be adapted to wool, by the use of mordants already known to the people and formerly used for cotton, even though such dyes may require different adjustments in treatment for the new fiber.

However, it is certain that the Hopi, lineal descendants of the prehistoric basket makers of this region, still use, with equal success upon either wool or cotton, and other plant fibers, most of the old dyes. The shades produced, however, vary considerably on the various fibers.

The introduction of aniline dyes about 1880* was a severe check upon the native dye industry, both Hopi and Navajo, though it

* Amsden, 1934, p. 88.

would seem that native dyes never came as near complete extinction among the Hopi as with the Navajo. This, however, has not been fully realized, owing to the fact that there are so few Hopi textiles on the market and that the Hopi carry on an extensive intertribal trade.

The revival of Indian arts in the 1930's, for which the Museum of Northern Arizona has been working among the Hopi, has stimulated the people to renewed interest in their ancient crafts and to a lively experimentation with dyes and mordants.

Transcribing Hopi words into English

The spelling of Hopi words with our English alphabet offers some difficulties. We have adopted in this work the following rules: the vowels have continental values such as in German, French, or Spanish; the consonants, as in English, except *q* without *u* is used for *k* sound further back in the throat than the English *k*. The Hopi language has no *b, d, g, rz,* or *sh,* and it distinguishes between long and short vowels: between short vowels, *a* and between long vowels, *a:*. A glottal stop is ' and an accent is '.

CHAPTER II

Textile and Basketry Objects

THE FOLLOWING ARTICLES were being manufactured in the pueblos in 1954, but no claim is made that this is a complete list.

Textiles Worn by Women

1. Wedding robe: hand spun white cotton, basket weave.
2. Wedding belt: hand spun white cotton, braided.
3. Maiden's shawl: white wool or cotton with red border, diagonal basket weave.
4. Woman's ceremonial dress: made from small wedding robe and heavily embroidered in colored wool yarns.
5. Woman's dress: diamond, diagonal weave, dark blue and black.
6. Woman's belt: red, floated patterns in black and green.
7. Woman's (sometimes men's) footless stockings or leggings: black or white; knit in several patterns by the men.

Textiles Worn by Small Children (textiles for children are always black and white)

8. Baby's blanket: wool, basket weave.
9. Boy's shoulder blanket: two sizes, black and white plaid design, basket weave.

Textiles Worn by Men

10. Ceremonial sash: wool or cotton, basket weave, brocaded in colored wools.
11. Ceremonial kilt: hand spun white cotton, basket weave, heavily embroidered in colored wool yarns.
12. Shirts and kilts: blue or black wool, basket weave.
13. Hair tie: cotton warp, red, floated patterns in green and white.

4

14. Garters: cotton or wool warp, red or black, floated patterns in black, white, red and green.
15. Wearing blanket: wool, soft loose weave, broad and fine stripes in many colors. (Worn with stripes in vertical position—shoulder blanket.)
16. Chief blanket: heavy wool blanket, tapestry weave, broad stripes of white, blue and red or orange, with design in center, and corners; worn horizontally.
17. Shoulder blanket: black and white plaid, twilled basket weave.

Household Textiles

18. Bed blanket: soft, loosely woven wool blanket, stripes in many colors, larger than wearing blanket.
19. Rabbit skin blanket: twining, or finger weaving.
20. Cotton and wool blankets: diamond weave.
21. Rugs: tapestry weave, Kachina design, or copy of Navajo.

Leather Work

22. Wedding boots: white doe skin, knee height, puttee tops, wound about the leg and tied.
23. Men's and women's low moccasins with tongues: buckskin dyed red, rawhide sole stitched with tendon.

Basketry (vegetable dyes and natural colors in many hues)

24. Oraibi wicker plaque (lump center).
25. Oraibi wicker shallow ceremonial plaque basket.
26. Oraibi wicker deep basket (modern forms).
27. Second Mesa coiled plaque.
28. Second Mesa coiled shallow ceremonial basket.
29. Second Mesa coiled deep basket (modern forms).

Utility Basketry, Natural Colors

30. Yucca winnowing basket.
31. Yucca deep basket.
32. Burden basket of wicker.
33. Piki tray, wicker.
34. Head cover for cradle board.
35. Cradle.
36. Matting door cover.
37. Grass bundle tied with yucca for door covers.

CHAPTER III

Cotton and Its History

COTTON IS A FIBER CLOTHING the seeds in the pods of certain shrubs and trees growing in tropical and semi-tropical countries and in various parts of western and southern United States where conditions are favorable for its culture.

The Hopi Indians originally grew their own cotton, native to parts of Arizona, a special species called *Gossypium hopi.** This cotton until recently was, and may be still, grown in small quantities to be used in ceremonies and hand spun. At the present time the Hopi use commercial cotton batting or usually cotton string for work in their textiles.

The color of cotton varies from deep yellow to white. The fiber differs in length, the long stapled being the most valued.

Cotton, unlike wool, requires special preparation for dyeing, as its fibers are water repellent. It is not washed with soap or yucca suds like wool, but must be boiled gently in plain water until thoroughly wetted and softened and the air bubbles pressed out.

There are two main methods of procedure, either of which may be followed in the dyeing of cotton.

Method 1

The first is that which is now used by the Hopi. Cotton is dyed and mordanted in one simple process; the mordanting agent being in the dye, into which the boiled spun cotton is immersed.

The method used by the Hopi is as follows:

After the spun cotton has been gently boiled, to soften and wet the fibers, it is lightly wrung or pressed out and immediately

* Whiting, 1939, p. 84.

immersed in the dye, which has already been mordanted. (See directions in recipes.) It is then boiled for a short period and set aside, in the dye, to soak for at least 24 hours. The one exception to this procedure will be found in the recipe for dyeing with natural indigo which is *not* boiled but soaked after the cotton is immersed in the dye.

Method 2

In the second method, the cotton is mordanted or prepared to receive the dye, previous to dyeing. These processes are varied and elaborate. The cotton is usually boiled or soaked in an astringent containing tannic acid, for which cotton has a natural affinity. This, in combination with other mordants and chemicals in the dyes, precipitates the coloring matter and fixes it in the fibers.

There are many variations in the mordanting and preparation of cotton for the dye bath, and in some cases the process is reversed and the cotton is soaked in an alum bath first and afterward boiled in an astringent solution of tannic acid.

Mordants

Tannic acid is contained in many plants and shrubs. (See Chapter V, mordants.) Stale urine, sheep manure, and the smoke of various plants and animal fibers have all been used as mordants from very ancient times all over the world.

CHAPTER IV

Wool and Its History

WOOL FIBERS are composed of a central cellular marrow called the medulla, which is incased in a substance composed of elongated conical cells, called the cortex, while the surface of the fiber is covered by rough epidermal scales.

These scales consist of a horny translucent substance, closely overlapping and varying in form according to the type of wool.

Reaction to moisture, heat and color

Wool fibers are extremely hydroscopic and when soaked in cold water, gradually soften and swell. When warm water or hot water is used, the process is accelerated. The epidermal scales open out and the fibers become gelatinous and temporarily lose their elasticity. In this state wool fibers show a greater affinity for dye stuffs. After washing and drying, therefore, wool should always be steeped in lukewarm water before immersing in a dye bath.

The above reactions may be studied under the microscope, when the physical changes, taking place in the fibers subjected to various treatments, can be clearly observed.

Wool, if subjected to high temperatures, either by long continued boiling or by dry heat, gradually decomposes.

Action of acids and alkalis

Wool is unaffected by dilute acids; in fact, it has a great affinity for them. But wool, being an animal fiber, is tendered and weakened by strong alkalis and when used in concentrated form they will completely dissolve it. Soaps containing caustic alkalis should never be used upon wool. Dilute alkalis are effective cleansing agents and may be used with care.

The best type of wool for native spinning and dyeing is the fleece of the "unimproved" or "old type" Navajo sheep.* This wool is long, loosely waved and comparatively free from lanoline or "wool fat." It is, therefore, easily scoured by the usual Indian method, with the pounded root of the yucca and cold or lukewarm water, instead of modern soap and hot water, which is essential for all "improved" or grease wools. In fact, this wool is so free of grease, and therefore contains so little dirt, that even today it is often not washed at all before dyeing, but is carefully selected and the dirt thoroughly shaken out. Formerly, this was a general custom among the Navajo, due to the scarcity of water.† However, if this yarn is to be used as white yarn and not dyed, or is to be dyed in indigo, it is always thoroughly scoured with yucca suds.

Wool to be used for dyeing and spinning is carefully selected from the shoulder and back of the fleece. This wool is usually the longest, finest and cleanest portion of the fleece. Stained wool from the lower and rear portion of the body of the sheep and the out-side coarse, "hair-like" ends of the Navajo or "unimproved wools" are usually discarded. However, from the Hopi of Second Mesa, we have information that some weavers claim that the stained wool has a decided affinity for certain dyes and should be used without scouring as richer and more permanent shades can thus be pro-duced. The writer has checked this information in the laboratory and finds it essentially correct.

How wool may be washed and dyed without shrinking

Extremes of heat and cold and violent changes of temperature have a tendency to shrink wool. Wool should be washed in luke-warm water at a temperature not higher than 100° F. and its rinse water should be of a similar temperature. In other words, it should not be subjected to violent changes of temperature during washing and scouring.

If this wool is to be dyed, the dye bath should also be lukewarm when the material is ready to be immersed. When the wool has been immersed in the lukewarm dye bath, it must be brought to a boil slowly and kept boiling at a low temperature.

When wool is to be dried after washing, or after it has been dyed, it should be dried in a warm room or outdoors in the sun.

* Colton, 1932.
† Amsden, 1934.

Ironing woolen material or subjecting it to freezing after washing will cause it to shrink badly.

Wool before dyeing: Wool that has been washed and allowed to dry before dyeing should be steeped or soaked in warm water for half an hour or so before immersing it in the dye bath. This will remove the air from the wool and soften it, so that it will take the dye more evenly.

Treatment of unwashed wool before dyeing: Wool that is to be used unwashed for dyeing, is carefully selected for its lack of grease and stain and is called "dry wool" because it feels dry to the touch, rather than cold and wet, like the grease wools. I have been informed that "dry wool" is usually chosen from the ewes.

After selection, this wool is carefully shaken out and it is then soaked for a few minutes in cold or lukewarm water, like dry washed wool, before immersing it in the dye bath.

Two native methods of cleaning wool

Washing wool with the suds of yucca root, narrow leaved or Hopi *mohu*, is practiced by both Navajo and Hopi.

The Navajo generally used cold water for this operation, while the Hopi seemed to prefer lukewarm water, saying that it makes better suds.

If the wool is very heavily laden with dirt and sand, it will first have the burs and sticks picked out and as much of the loose sand shaken free as possible. It will then be washed and steeped in plain water several times before the actual scouring begins.

Washing wool with white earth, or Hopi "Fullers earth,"* seems to have originated among the Hopi people, where this white earth is plentiful under their sandstone mesas.

However, I am told that certain Navajo also use the "white earth method" and that it is believed that they have copied it from the Hopi.

Washing and cleansing of wool: The Hopi, like the Navajo, has always used the root of the *Yucca angustifolia* or soap weed (several other types may be used for suds). It is prepared in the following manner.

The root of the yucca, which is about 18 inches long, is dug from the ground. It is a fibrous, tough, yellow substance, full of

* A colloidal alumnar sulphate.

a rather glutinous sap. These roots are pounded with a rock until the fibers are separated and torn apart.

A bowl of water is then warmed over the fire (or cold water is used) and the fibrous, pounded yucca root is placed in it and worked with the hands until a fine white suds is obtained. The yucca is then squeezed out and put away for future use. It may be used several times, after re-pounding, although the root is much more effective when fresh. It is used in cold water, but seems most effective in warm water (as the Hopi use it). It is slightly astringent.

Unimproved Navajo wool, washed once in yucca suds and then rinsed in warm water comes out a beautiful white, very light and fluffy.

Washing wool with white earth or Hopi "Fullers earth": The people of both Second and Third Mesas agree that this chalky white substance from the sandstone layers under the Mesas near their towns, acts as an excellent cleanser for both woolen and cotton stuffs. It is often used in place of yucca root. In fact, I am told that many women prefer it to yucca root. I have also been told that the Navajo adopted this cleansing method from the Hopi.

The wool or material to be washed, is carried to the spring and spread out on a flat rock nearby where it is sprinkled with the white powdered chalky earth. It is then thoroughly wet down with water and is kneaded and worked until the white earth is thoroughly mixed with the wool; it may or may not be rinsed. If it is to be spun and woven into a blanket, it probably will not be rinsed but merely dried and shaken out. Blankets, woolen dresses, etc., and also cotton goods, are washed in this way. This earth rinses out nicely and leaves the wool very white, soft and clean, and free of grease. This method has also been tested by the writer and the results on the "dry" or greaseless wool of the native sheep are excellent, but not as satisfactory on the "improved" wools, Rambouillet and crosses, which carry a heavy load of sticky grease.

The blood of the French Merino or Rambouillet has been extensively introduced by the government into the flocks of both Navajo and Hopi. These crosses have produced a type of wool entirely unsuitable for hand spinning and weaving. The fleece of merino types is heavily laden with a sticky grease called "wool fat" or lanoline, which renders it almost impossible for the Indian to scour properly with the primitive methods to which he is accustomed. This wool is extremely short, closely packed and sharply crimped. It carries an immense load of dirt embedded in the "wool fat."

Wool for hand spinning and weaving has requirements quite different from those for the machine. For the modern machine it is the fineness of the wool fiber that is of first importance, not the length, and a sharp crimp is not a disadvantage, as the machine is constructed to straighten this, and wools such as merino, heavily laden with grease, are easily cleaned by commercial methods.

Treatment of wool before dyeing

On this matter there seems to be a variety of opinions. An Oraibi informant tells us that the wool is always washed carefully with the suds of yucca root before being carded and spun, even brown wool, which is used instead of white, when a good black dye is desired. He has never seen unwashed wool dyed.

However, the same informant says that he has heard a rumor of wool being soaked in liquid sheep manure before dyeing. He thinks this may be something recent. ("Recent," among Indian peoples, may mean a matter of several hundred years.) He has also heard of rock salt being used as a mordant for dyes, but he does not know what particular dyes. This informant says cotton is never washed or wet before carding and spinning, because it mats up and this makes it hard to work with.

A Second Mesa informant says that wool sometimes is not washed at all, but only shaken out to free it of sand. He has seen this done particularly where the wool is to be dyed with "aniline dyes," especially the deep maroon red. This dyer believes that the dye "takes better" on the unwashed wool. Where wool is to be dyed with *hohoi'si* or *si:'ita* vegetable dyes, he says that it is first soaked in liquid sheep manure. All informants agree that wool is always carefully washed in yucca suds before dyeing it in indigo. The Second Mesa informant also states that cotton (perhaps after spinning), is almost always soaked in liquid sheep manure before dyeing and he thinks this may have been used as a mordant for wool also.

The Second Mesa informant says that when unwashed wool is dyed, the wool from the under parts of the animal is chosen, that which is stained by urine and manure in the corrals when the animal lies down.

The Oraibi informant does not know of this, although he states that this kind of wool is always used to smoke basketry and yarn.

It is probable that human urine, fermented, was used as a mordant in which to soak cotton before the introduction of domestic animals.

From these opinions, some idea of the latitude in native dyeing practices can be obtained.

The reasons for this are several, the principal being, that the Hopi have never had a "written language." Various clans and individuals use different methods.

It is interesting to note that all these opinions have precedent in early practices in other parts of the world. In India, cotton is mordanted with cow dung.

CHAPTER V

Mordants, Chemicals and Measures

A MORDANT IS A CHEMICAL used to precipitate the active principal of the dye in the fiber. The mordant is said to fix or set the color and make the dye insoluble in water or water with neutral soaps. Mordants are used in two ways; either mixed with the dye or the textile is dipped in a mordant bath before or after the dye bath.

Common native Hopi mordants
1. Crude native alum from efflorescence of drying soil.
2. Limonite from Chinle or Mancos Shale.
3. Rock salt from Zuni Salt Lake or Grand Canyon.
4. Copper carbonate from copper ore from Verde Valley.
5. Cream-of-tarter, potassium tartrate.
6. Tannic acid from sumac (Rhus trilobata) berries, branches or leaves.
7. Lye made from wood ashes.
8. Human urine.
9. Sheep manure and water, filtered.
10. Smoke.
11. Iron tannate soot produced by burning pinyon gum with native ochre.

>   Soluble in water 20.24%
>   Total iron   5.68%
>   Total sulphate   14.56%

12. "Potato Clay." This is a nickeliferous talc containing a small amount of aluminum.

Hopi Measures

Handfuls and double handfuls; their equivalent in grams and litres or millilitres, or cc.

Dry Measure: The measure by handfuls can be used for wool, cotton, indigo, whole plants and plant blossoms. These vary somewhat, a handful of cotton, plants and plant blossoms being lighter in weight than wool or indigo. In measuring these materials in handfuls, fill the hands, stuff, and press tightly together.

	Measures
1 small double handful, wool	30-40 grams
1 large double handful, cotton	30-40 grams
4 double handfuls	160 grams
1 double handful	40 grams
2 double handfuls	80 grams
1 single handful	2.5 grams

Handfuls and double handfuls, their equivalent in litres or millilitres. These vary as much as 25 ml. This measure can be used for corn, beans, sunflower seed, sumac berries or other seeds —alum, salt, iron powder, copper carbonate, and powdered ochre.

	Measures
1 small single handful	25 ml.
1 large single handful	75 ml.
1 small double handful	100 ml.
1 large double handful	150 ml.
2 double handfuls	300 ml.
3 double handfuls	450 ml.
5 double handfuls	750 ml.
6 double handfuls	900 ml.

Liquid Measure: Quarts and cups — their equivalent in litres or millilitres, rough measure.

1 litre	1 quart or 4 cups
1½ litres	1 quart and 1 pint or 6 cups
2 litres	2 quarts or 8 cups
4 litres	4 quarts or 16 cups
150 ml.	½ cup
200 ml.	¾ cup
300 ml.	1-1/3 cups

Secondary Mordants — Smoking

The Hopi have always practiced smoking as a method of "setting the color" in various dyed materials.

It is used for basketry materials and for wool, also for cotton yarns to a lesser extent.

In the case of several dyes, smoking is relied upon to cause a complete chemical change in the color of the dyed materials, while in others, it serves only to intensify the shade and "set" the color.

Methods and materials used for the smoking of dyes: A fire of juniper wood is made, and allowed to burn down to embers. Dirty greasy wool is the material commonly used to place upon the charcoal, smothering the fire and thus causing a dense smoke. This wool is chosen from the underside and rear of the sheep and is soaked with urine and sheep manure, thus the thick yellow smoke produced contains a large amount of ammonia and other chemicals.

This smoke is very powerful as the writer has learned, inhalation of it having caused a severe attack of laryngitis.

At other times, corncobs are used, but the writer has not so far been able to ascertain whether this is always for a particular dye, or to take the place of the wool. Certainly they do not have the same chemical effect.

Smoking is sometimes done over an open fire, but in most cases, large storage jars, or tin wash boilers, are rigged up to contain the hot coals and wool, and so arranged that there is a draft at the bottom, and a method of suspending the material, whether basketry or yarn, over the smoking wool and coals. This contrivance is fitted with a top of some sort to control the smoke and to attain a maximum efficiency.

For the present experimenter, the "wash boiler" method, copied from an old lady in Oraibi, has proved most efficient.

The boiler has a row of holes about 2 or 3 inches from the bottom all around it, a wire rack for the material three-quarters of the way up, and a top which may be tilted in any direction to allow a good draft. The charcoal is produced in a fire nearby and transferred to the bottom of the boiler which is elevated from the ground upon stones.

Dirty wool, as described, is immediately placed over the live coals and produces a prodigious yellow smoke. The material at hand is then spread wet upon the wire rack, which is placed over the smoke, and the top is adjusted. Every few minutes the material is examined and turned about. If wool or cotton, the maximum effect will not be attained until the material has completely dried in the smoker.

However, no definite time can be given for smoking. Judgement and experience are required for the best results and the material is removed when the desired shade is obtained.

Dark brown or black wool is commonly used for the smoking of dark colors and white wool for light colors. This, however, the writer feels, has no real effect upon the results.

Soaps and Scouring Agents

Many vegetable dyes have a totally different reaction upon material washed with different scouring agents and soaps.

These scouring agents seem to act to some extent, as lesser mordants in themselves, causng the mordanted dyes to produce different shades upon materials scoured with the various agents.

The group of lavender, purple and carmine dyes, derived from starchy seeds, such as corn, beans and sunflower seed, are particularly influenced by the type of scouring agent used.

Upon wool washed with yucca suds, these dyes tend toward the red-purples, but on wool washed with a neutral soap such as Lux or Ivory, they develop a more bluish tone.

When this group of dyes is washed with soaps after dyeing, they almost all turn much more bluish.

The Hopi's present knowledge of complicated mordanting principles, which seem to be, with a few exceptions, tried more or less experimentally upon various plants in their present habitat, suggests that their art is very old, but that it has been transported in fairly recent times, perhaps hundreds of years, at least in part, to a new region with an unfamiliar flora.

It is felt that the present situation distinctly suggests a period of greater stabilization and a present deterioration of the dyer's art.

This may be partially due to the introduction of wool by the Spaniards in 1640, a new fiber to the Hopi, upon which many of the ancient dyes were not effective and, therefore, necessitating much additional experimentation.

CHAPTER VI

Preparation of Textiles for Dyeing

AFTER THE HOPI INDIAN has prepared his cotton or wool for dyeing, as described in the past few chapters, the material is ready for the dye bath. These dye baths are different for the different vegetable dyes, and in the following chapters the preparations of stock solutions are described and each stock solution may be further treated in different ways called recipes.

In making up these stock solutions and recipes the material is measured out. As the Indians do not have scales to weigh out ingredients or other measures they use single handfuls or double handfuls or cups to measure quantities. Cotton or wool have about the same specific gravity so that a single handful weighs about 25 grams and a double handful weighs about 40 grams. For a fluid measure the Indian uses teacups; four cups equal about a quart or a litre.

The classification of stock solutions and recipes is based on color (a) from the red to gold and red-brown, (b) gold to yellow, (c) blue, (d) purple, and (e) black.

In some cases the dyed material has been tested for fading or for washing with soap.

Interesting ceremonial customs are connected with the gathering of dye plants as well as many strange superstitions.

Before a man goes out into the country to gather plants for his dyes, he makes a prayer to each particular kind of plant.

If a woman is pregnant, she must be very careful not to "run in" on a man or woman who is doing dye work, for if she does, the color will not take on the material. The only thing that she can do to help, if this has happened, is to apologize to the dyer and then spit into the dye pot, when everything will at once be well.

On the other hand, if a pregnant woman is doing some dye work herself and a neighbor comes in, it will spoil the dyer's work. But worst of all, if a man has been in a house where someone has died or has helped to bury a friend, should he then happen in on a dyer at work, it will cause all his dyed material to fade. There is nothing that can be done about this.

In comparing Navajo dye plants used by Mrs. Bryan* with the Hopi plants and dye materials, only three plants are used by the Hopi and not by the Navajo. There are also three plants used by both Hopi and Navajo and twenty-four plants are mentioned as used by Mrs. Bryan that were not mentioned by the Hopi informants.

Since the Hopi and Navajo Indians occupy similar environments, one would naturally expect them to use the same resources, but in regard to dye plants the Hopi do not use many of those used by Mrs. Bryan, a Navajo.

* Bryan and Young, 1940.

Common Name	Hopi Name	Scientific Reference
Blue Kidney Bean	*tupenmori*	*Phaseolus vulgaris*
Canaigre	*saya'vi*	*Rumex hymenosephalus*
Fetid Marigold	*tu'i'tsma*	*Pectis angustifolia*
Greenthread	*hohoi'si*	*Thelesperma megapotamicum*
Goldenrod	*na'palnga*	*Solidago* sp.
Mountain Mahogany	*putci'vi*	*Cercocarpus breviflorus* var. *eximius*
Navajo Tea	*si:'ta*	*Thelesperma subnudum*
Purple Corn	*koko'ma*	*Zea mays amylacea*
Rabbit Brush	*siva'pi*	*Chrysothamnus* sp.
Sumac	*su:'vi*	*Rhus trilobata*
Sunflower	*'a:'gaw'u*	*Helianthus* sp.

HOPI DYE COLOR GROUPS

Colors	Dyeing Items	Color Ranges
reds	Purple Corn	carmine-pink
carmines		carmine-reds
madders		raspberry-red
maroons		maroon-red
		deep maroon-red
purple	Sunflower	deep maroon
lavender	(black-seeded)	purple
		deep lavender
vermillion	Greenthread	vermillion
apricot	Navajo Tea	vermillion
pink	Canaigre	apricot-pink
rust red	Greenthread	rust
Indian red	Navajo Tea	Indian reds
orange-gold	Greenthread	red-orange
	Canaigre	deep gold
burnt orange	Greenthread	burnt orange
yellows	Canaigre	deep gold
golds	Fetid Marigold	gold shades
	Greenthread	deep golds
	Rabbit Brush (tall)	bright gold

| | Rabbit Brush (blossoms, recipe #4) | green-gold |
| | Goldenrod | bright gold |

lemon yellow	Rabbit Brush (blossoms, stems)	green-yellows
	Rabbit Brush (second size)	green-yellows
	Rabbit Brush (tall)	pale yellow

| ochre yellow | Ochre | brown-earth |
| | Mineral Yellow | yellows |

greens	Indigo (recipe #2)	dark green
	Indigo (recipe #1)	deep green
	Indigo (immature plants)	pale green
	Indigo (stems, leaves)	pale green
	Indigo (blossoms, second size)	yellow-green
	Indigo (blossoms)	gold-green

blues	Indigo Blue	deep blue
	Purple Corn	lavender-blue
	Sunflower Seed	medium blue
	Blue Kidney Bean	blue, purple-blue

purple	Purple Corn	bright purple
	Blue Kidney Bean	purples
lavenders	Sunflower Seed (black)	lavender-blue
	Sunflower Seed	dark purple

tans	Purple Corn	tan
brown	Purple Corn Cobs	red-browns
	Mountain Mahogany (bark)	rust-brown

| black | No. 1 - Iron Tannate (mixture of pinyon gum, ochre and black seeded sunflower.) | black |
| | No. 2 - Iton Tannate (mixture of pinyon gum, ochre and sumac leaves.) | black |

CHAPTER VII

Reds and Golds and Red-browns

FETID MARIGOLD *tu'i'tsma (Pectis angustifolia)*

Tu'ı'ᴛsᴍᴀ is an inconspicuous plant with fine composite yellow blossoms. When mature, it is about 4 inches high and has a delicious "lemon verbena" odor. It grows in the sand dunes near the Hopi mesas. The whole plant is gathered while in blossom and used at once or dried for future use.*

This plant is not as highly valued as the thelespermas, as it is capable of producing one color only, an old gold shade, somewhat similar to that produced by *si:'ta* before smoking.

Its color is not materially altered by smoking or the use of acids or strong alkalis. We have no record of its use by the Navajo or other tribes and therefore, believe that it is peculiar to the Hopi alone.

Tu'i'tsma is equally effective on basketry, cotton or wool. It is used today upon all three. It is used upon the Third Mesa wicker material but not upon the Second Mesa yucca basketry material.

Its preparation is simple. The plants are packed into a kettle and well covered with water. This is brought slowly to a boil and kept boiling gently for several hours, refilling when necessary. It is then removed from the fire and strained through a cloth and squeezed out thoroughly. The resulting liquid is a clear yellow-brown.

Ground or melted native alum is then added to the liquid, which at once turns a rich, opaque old gold.

The mixture is replaced on the fire and allowed to boil for a few minutes. It is then ready to receive the material to be dyed.

* Whiting, 1939, p. 97.

For the dyeing of basketry material, the dye bath may be brought to the boiling point, but not allowed to boil after the material has been immersed. The dye is placed in a receptacle sufficiently long to accommodate the prepared *siva'pi* (rabbit brush) stems, either loose or tied in small bundles. There should be sufficient dye to cover the material and the pan should be rocked at intervals and the bundles turned to insure the dye taking evenly upon all the material.

The material is removed when it has attained the desired shade, and is placed damp in the smoker. Sometimes it is smoked and then dipped again and this process may be repeated several times to increase the depth of the shade.

FETID MARIGOLD
TU'I'TSMA GOLD

Stock Dye No. 1*

Use blossoming, whole plants, 4 inches high.

4 double handfuls (100 grams) of plants. Place in 4-quart kettle and cover with water, 16 cups (4 litres).

Bring to boil slowly. Boil 1-2 hours gently. Refill when necessary.

Reduce to 8 cups (2 litres).

Strain through cotton cloth; squeeze out well.

Result: Clear, yellow-brown liquid.

* A stock dye is a dye solution before mordanting.

Recipe No. 1   FETID MARIGOLD   For wool and cotton
TU'I'TSMA GOLD
tu'i'tsma (Pectis angustifolia)

Use Stock Dye No. 1.

Mordanting: Take 1 small double handful (100 ml.) of native alum. Pour into hot iron frying pan. Sprinkle with little water, melt down and pour into dye, which at once turns to rich, deep, opaque gold. This plant yields a large amount of rich color.

Material added: Into 8 cups (2 litres) of dye immerse 1 double handful (30-40 grams) of wool washed in yucca suds or cotton soaked in hot water.

Treatment in dye: Boil 1-2 hours.

After treatment: Soak overnight. Remove, wring slightly and dry. Rinse thoroughly.

Result: Wool — a clear, light, old gold; cotton — boiled 1 hour in dye; result: fine, deep, old gold. Soaked overnight, results the same.

(Maerz and Paul, 12-L-5, Light stone L)*

* Color determinations have been made for some recipes, based on the Maerz and Paul system of color identification.

Recipe No. 2   FETID MARIGOLD   For wool and cotton
                      TU'I'TSMA GOLD
                tu'ï'tsma (Pectis angustifolia)

Use Stock Dye No. 1.

Mordanting: Add to this dye 1 small double handful (100 ml.) of ground native alum. Liquid at once turns rich, opaque gold.

Material added: Into 8 cups (2 litres) of this dye, immerse 1 double handful (30-40 grams) of unwashed wool or cotton which has been soaked 24 hours in strong liquid sheep manure. Remove, wring slightly and place damp in dye.

Treatment in dye: Boil 1 hour or more.

After treatment: Remove, wring slightly. Immerse damp in urine and work for a few minutes. Wring and dry. Rinse thoroughly.

Result: Brilliant old gold on both wool and cotton; cotton slightly darker. Urine both enriches color appreciably and adds to permanency.
(Maerz and Paul, wool, 11-L-7, Yelow Ochre P; cotton, 13-L-9, Chipmunk.)

Recipe No. 3   FETID MARIGOLD   For wool and cotton
                      TU'I'TSMA GOLD
                tu'ï'tsma (Pectis angustifolia)

Use Stock Dye No. 1.

Mordanting: Add to this dye 1 small double handful (100 ml.) of ground native alum. Liquid at once turns rich, opaque gold.

Material added: Into 8 cups (2 litres) of this dye immerse 1 double handful (30-40 grams) of unwashed natural wool, dampened, or cotton that has been soaked in boiling water.

Treatment in dye: Bring to a boil and simmer gently for 1 hour or more.

After treatment: Remove, wring slightly. Immerse damp in urine bath and work for a few minutes. Rinse in several waters. Wring lightly and dry.

Result: Good shade of old gold on wool; poor on cotton.
(Maerz and Paul, 12-L-6, Tennis)

Additional experiment tried: Test: Washed in Lux soap — good, light gold; then run through urine bath — deep gold.

Recipe No. 4   FETID MARIGOLD   For wool and cotton
                        TU'I'TSMA GOLD
                    tu'i'tsma (Pectis angustifolia)

Material: Tu'i'tsma, mature blossoming plants 4 inches high. 100
   grams plants. 15 ml. water.

Mordanting: Boil 3 hours and strain; liquid yellow-brown. Put 1
   double handful (50 grams) of native alum in hot iron frying
   pan, sprinkle a little water on alum; melt down alum at once
   and pour into dye. Dye turns a deep old gold.

Material added: Put in wool, yucca washed; cotton, plain boiled.

Treatment in dye: Boil cotton in dye 1 hour. Boil wool in dye 2
   hours and soak overnight; rinse wool.

Result: Wool, clear, light, old gold. Lime water and ammonia do
   not alter this color. Cotton, a fine, permanent, old gold, washed.

GOLDS AND REDS
hohoi'si* *(Thelesperma megapotamicum)*
si:'ta* *(Thelesperma subnudum)*

Habitat, character and properties as dyes

These two little plants, closely related, are of great interest. Of all the Hopi dye plants, they are capable of producing the richest and most permanent shades.

The Hopi value them highly and apparently they are used only by them, as we have no evidence that either of these plants are used by the Navajo or other tribes today. However, many well preserved Puebloan specimens of prehistoric cotton cloth from northern Arizona and the Verde Valley, closely match the shades produced today from these plants, so that we strongly feel that these dyes have indeed come a long way, and are very ancient favorites.

The thelespermas, *hohoi'si* and *si:'ta,* are both inconspicuous an-nual plants growing in sandy soil in certain restricted locations, particularly around the base of the Hopi mesas, at an altitude of about 4,500 feet. *Hohoi'si* may attain a height of 2 feet while *si:'ta* averages about 6 inches.

When these small plants first appear, they are difficult to differentiate. They yield the richest dye if gathered before the first rains, when only several inches high. If rain falls at this stage and the plants are examined immediately after the shower, it will be seen that there is a small blot of color in the sand, at the base of the young plants. Therefore, the careful Hopi weaver will gather the young plants before the rains, when they contain the maximum sap, and dry them for future use.

The small daisy-like composite flowers of the mature *hohoi'si* are also very effective as dye and are gathered and dried for use. The mature plants of both the thelespermas may be used, but the dye content is not as rich as in either the immature plants or the flowers.

The minute clusters of composite flowers of the *si:'ta* cannot conveniently be separated from the small plants which never attain a height of more than 6 inches. Therefore, the whole of this plant, flowers and all, is used in this case.

* Whiting, 1939, p. 98.

Both thelespermas yield rich shades ranging from deep old gold to brilliant orange-red, depending upon the stage in which the plant is gathered and the mordanting and treatment of the dye.

Both these dyes are sensitive to strong alkalis and their colors may be completely altered by the ammonia in the smoke of burning wool, or by immersion in a bath of stale urine (ammonia).

These dyes are equally effective upon cotton and wool or upon basketry material, and they are used today upon all three.

Both wicker and yucca basketry materials are dyed with these plants.

Preparation and Dyeing Process

The preparation of these dyes is simple. Either the green or dried plants or flowers are packed into a kettle and covered with a generous quantity of water. This is brought slowly to a boil and boiled gently for an hour or so. More water is added as necessary.

When it is removed from the fire, the liquid is strained through a cloth or fine strainer and the plants well squeezed out.

The result is a very rich, rather cloudy, red-brown liquid. Ground native alum is added to this, turning it a fine, opaque Indian red.

Replace the dye on the stove and bring it to a boil. When it has boiled for a few minutes, remove and let it cool slightly. It is now ready to receive the prepared damp wool or cotton.

(1) For light shades of old gold and tan, wool and cotton should not be smoked after dyeing.

(2) For deep shades of red-brown, both cotton and wool are smoked as described in the chapter on this process.

(3) To produce very intense shades of orange-red or vermilion, the dyed material, when removed from the dye pot and wrung out, may be placed in a solution of stale urine and worked in this for a few minutes. A very brilliant shade results. (See Recipe No. 2.)

When removed from the urine bath, the material should be thoroughly rinsed in several waters, and dried in the sun. The Hopi practice of smoking both these thelesperma dyes is used today, however, we have no authority, other than a strong suspicion, founded upon usage and colors which we have seen produced, that the Hopi made use of the urine bath for this plant, although it is used in many other cases.*

For the dyeing of basketry material see page 22.

* Used by Navajo (Bryan and Young, 1940, p. 69).

GOLDS AND REDS
hohoi'si (Thelesperma megapotamicum)

Stock Dye No. 1

Use blossoms.

1 large double handful (40 grams) *hohoi'si* blossoms, 8 cups (2 litres) of water. Bring to a boil slowly; boil gently 2 hours, adding water when necessary. Reduce to 6 cups (1½ litres). Strain through cotton cloth. Squeeze out.

Result: Clear, rich, dark brown liquid. These blossoms yield a very rich dye.

Stock Dye No. 2

Use mature, whole plants, without blossoms.

2 double handfuls (80 grams) *hohoi'si* plants. Place in 4-quart kettle and cover with 12 cups (2 litres) of water. Bring to boil slowly. Boil gently 4 hours, adding water as necessary. Reduce to 8 cups (2 litres). Strain through cotton cloth. Squeeze out.

Result: A dirty, brown-colored liquid.

Recipe No. 1   GREENTHREAD   For wool and cotton
                                OLD GOLD
          hohoi'si (Thelesperma megapotamicum)
Use Stock Dye No. 1.

Mordanting: Add to this dye 1 small double handful (100 ml.) of
     ground native alum. Dye at once turns opaque, yellow-brown.

Material added: Into 6 cups (1½ litres) of this dye, immerse 1
     double handful (30-40 grams) of wool washed in yucca suds
     and rinsed, or cotton soaked in hot water.

Treatment in dye: Bring to boil slowly and boil 1-2 hours.

After treatment: Remove and wring lightly and dry. Rinse thorough-
     ly.

Result: Wool, good, deep, old gold; cotton, somewhat redder.

Variation: Cotton may also be brought to boil in dye and then
     soaked for 24 hours.

Variations of Recipe No. 1

     (1) Smoked and then run through diluted ammonia water.
         Result: Good orange-gold or red-orange.
     (2) Wool washed in Lux or Ivory soap. Finished by smoking.
         Result: Good orange-gold.
     (3) Wool, Lux or Ivory washed. Finished by rinsing in diluted
         ammonia.
         Result: Clear orange-red.
     (4) Wool, Lux or Ivory washed. Finished by rinsing in diluted
         lye water.
         Result: Dull old gold.
     (5) Wool, Lux or Ivory washed.
         Result: Clear old gold.

Recipe No. 2   GREENTHREAD   NAVAJO TEA   For wool
HOHOI'SI VERMILION — SI:'TA VERMILION
(Thelesperma megapotamicum) — (Thelesperma subnudum)
Use recipes for *hohoi'si* and *si:'ta* yellow.

Mordanting: Dye yarn in *hohoi'si* or *si:'ta* yellow; rinse thoroughly. Now take urine which has been aged for 1 week and gives off a strong odor of ammonia, place this in a jar.

Material added: Immerse yellow *hohoi'si* or *si:'ta* dyed yarn into the stale urine.

Result: Yarn at once turns an intense shade of orange-scarlet. A very fine color. Dry yarn in shade in the open air.

Remarks: Aged urine when exposed to the air for any length of time, loses strength and this will cause the dyed gold yarn to take a longer time to turn vermilion in the urine bath.

Recipe No. 3   GREENTHREAD   For wool and cotton
ORANGE-RED
hohoi'si (Thelesperma megapotamicum)

Use Stock Dye No. 1 and Recipe No. 1.

When thelesperma gold material has been thoroughly rinsed, it is placed at once in stale urine, sufficient to completely cover material. It immediately turns a brilliant, rich orange-red. A very fine color. Allow it to steep at least 5 minutes. Remove and rinse several times in hot water and dry in sun.

Result: A very fine brilliant orange-red. It is also effective on cotton, but does not produce such a brilliant red.

Washing test: Wool, quite fast to washing; cotton, same.
(Maerz and Paul, 4-J-12, 4-K-12, Totem)

Recipe No. 4   GREENTHREAD   For wool and cotton
                            RED-BROWN
            hohoi'si (Thelesperma megapotamicum)

Use Stock Dye No. 1 and Recipe No. 3.

Smoking: When thelsperma gold *(hohoi'si)* material is removed
    from dye, and lightly wrung out, it is ready to be placed damp
    in smoker. Smoke about 1 hour, or until material is dry or
    desired shade of red-brown is reached.

Result: Wool, a fine Indian red; cotton, poor.
    (Maerz and Paul, 5-B-12, Cacao Brown)

Recipe No. 5   GREENTHREAD   For wool and cotton
                            PALE GOLD
            hohoi'si (Thelesperma megapotamicum)

Use Stock Dye No. 2.

Mordanting: Add to this 1 double handful (100 ml.) of native
    alum, previously melted in a hot iron pan, with a little water.
    Pour into dye liquid.

Material added: Into 4 cups (1 litre) immerse 1 single handful
    (25 grams) of wool washed in yucca suds and rinsed, or cotton
    soaked in hot water.

Treatment in dye: Bring to boil slowly and boil gently 3-4 hours
    in the dye.

After treatment: Remove, wring slightly, dry and rinse thoroughly.

Result: Wool, a very pale gold; cotton, a poor, dirty gold. Cotton
    much better when brought to a boil, then soaked overnight
    for 24 hours.
    (Maerz and Paul, 12-L-4, Sulphin Yellow R.)

Recipe No. 6   GREENTHREAD   For wool
BURNT ORANGE
hohoi'si (Thelesperma megapotamicum)

Use Stock Dye No. 2.

Add to 4 cups (1 litre) of water, 25 ml. of rock salt and immerse 1 single handful (25 grams) of wool. Boil 1 hour.

Remove, rinse and immerse again in Stock Dye No. 2. Boil 2 hours.

Result: Good, strong, gold color.

Variation: Run this wool through a bath of stale urine, rinse well and dry in sun.

Result: A fine, clear, burnt orange.

(Maerz and Paul, 13-A-12, Titian Gold)

Recipe No. 7   GREENTHREAD   For wool and cotton
HOHOI'SI GOLD
hohoi'si (Thelesperma megapotamicum)

Use mature *hohoi'si*, no blossoms.

Boil 2 double handfuls of plant in ¾ cup (200 ml.) of water 4 hours.

Add water from time to time as it evaporates. Liquid is a dirty brown color.

Mordanting: Add 50 grams of alum dissolved in water in pan to strained liquid.

Material added: Into 2 lots of this liquid, put Navajo wool washed in yucca, and wool boiled in rock salt. One lot, yucca washed, wool *very pale.*

Result: This dye turns orange with ammonia, like small *hohoi'si* plants and blossoms. Lot boiled in salt, then in dye, much stronger color. Smoked, turns brilliant Indian red. Cotton from both processes, pale and dull brown.

Recipe No. 8   GREENTHREAD   For wool

HOHOI'SI GOLD

hohoi'si (Thelesperma megapotamicum)

Use blossoms.

1 large handful (50 grams) blossoms.

8 cups (2 litres) water.

Bring to boil slowly and boil 2 hours.

Strain; liquor resulting is a clear dark brown.

Mordanting: Add 40 grams ground native alum; dye turns opaque yellow-brown.

Material added: Immerse Navajo wool washed in yucca and rinsed. Boil for 2 hours. Rinse and dry.

Result: A nice, golden orange.

Recipe No. 9   GREENTHREAD   For wool, cotton and basketry

HOHOI'SI RED

hohoi'si (Thelesperma megapotamicum)

Material added: Immerse this wool, (resulting from Recipe No. 8) into pure stale urine, 1 week old, smelling of ammonia.

Result: Hohoi'si yellow dyed wool at once turns an intense orange-scarlet. A wonderful color! *Si:'ta* will do the same. *Siva'pis* are not much affected by urine. Urine seems to lose strength when exposed to air and wool takes longer to turn red. When wool is finally washed twice in hot water it does not lose any color. Fresh urine will also change cotton or basket material to a nice red-orange. It does not work as rapidly and the result is not such a brilliant red.

GREENTHREAD OR NAVAJO TEA   For basketry
GOLDS AND REDS
hohoi'si or *si:'ta* (*Thelesperma* sp.)

Any of the recipes given under Thelesperma Golds and Reds may be used for basketry material, both yucca and peeled rabbit brush stems and quite possibly, other basketry fibers. These dyes are strong and the shades intense, they take readily both on animal and vegetable fibers.

Dyeing

In a receptacle long enough to accommodate the length of the material (10-12 inches) the mordanted dye is allowed to cool until nearly lukewarm. The stems or yucca strips, are immersed in this dye bath, either loose or in bundles tied lightly. The vessel is gently agitated at intervals and the bundles are turned so that the dye will take evenly on the material. The dye may be reheated during the process but never brought to a boil. The Navajo also use these plants.*

Smoking

If a bright orange or deep red-brown shade is desired, it will be smoked while still damp. The bundles of dyed basketry material should be placed in the smoker and smoked until the desired intensity or shade is obtained. It may be necessary to re-dip the material in the dye, which has been reheated several times during the smoking process. (See Chapter V.)

* Bryan and Young, 1940.

Dye experiment   MOUNTAIN MAHOGANY   For wool only
RED-BROWN

putci'vi (Cercocarpus breviflorus var. eximius)

Take 1 double handful of the bark of the root of the mountain mahogany. Place in a kettle and cover well with water. Boil this for about 2 hours or until liquid is a clear, deep, red-brown. Remove from fire and strain off liquid.

Mordanting: Take 1 handful native alum and boil down.

Material added: Pour off clear liquid, replace on fire and immerse yarn that has been soaked in warm water previously.

Treatment in dye: Boil yarn ½-¾ hour. Now remove yarn, wring lightly and place in dye. Boil gently for at least 2 hours.

After treatment: Remove yarn and wring lightly to dispose of extra dye.

Result: A good, strong, red-brown.

CHAPTER VIII

Yellows and Golds

siva'pi or Rabbit Brush *(Chrysothamnus sp.)*

Habitat, character and properties as a dye

THERE ARE MANY SPECIES of this handsome, well-known plant throughout the Southwest. They vary in size from 1 foot to 5 feet in height and all bear composite yellow blossoms. They are found in the high desert and foothill country. Four species are used in these recipes.

Because this plant is widely distributed geographically and its use as a dye is known to the Navajo* as well as the Hopi and possibly to other Indian peoples of the Southwest, it is felt that this could be classed as one of the older native dye stuffs. The Hopi use at least three or four varieties of this perennial plant.

Mature flowers are gathered when in their prime and either used at once or dried and stored in quantities for use during the coming winter.

If yellow-green is desired, immature blossoms are used or the pale green stems of the plant itself will produce a delicate shade of green.

Mature blossoms from the different varieties produce a series of shades, from lemon-yellow to a deep, golden color.

Siva'pi dye is equally effective upon cotton, wool, or basketry materials. It is in use among the Hopi today, upon all three. We have no recent record of its modern use upon cotton, as there is very little cotton dyeing done, except for ceremonial purposes.

The preparation of this dye is simple. It has one phase only, the

* Bryan and Young, 1940, p. 56.

alkaline. Native alum, aluminum sulphate, is the mordant in general use. This color appears unaffected by acids and is not sensitive to temperature changes.

Smoking or the "urine bath," only very slightly intensify the shade, though it is thought that either treatment has a tendency to render the color more permanent.

Exposure to sunlight or intense light, over a period of years, causes this dye to turn slightly brownish.

To dye wool

Wool should be placed damp in the warm mordanted dye bath and brought to a boil slowly and boiled gently for several hours, or until the desired shade is obtained.

To dye cotton

Cotton, like most vegetable fibers, takes the dye better when soaked, rather than boiled for a long period. However, it should first be placed damp in the mordanted dye bath and brought slowly to a boil and kept boiling for a few minutes, then it should be removed, set aside and soaked for 24 hours.

Basketry material, Third Mesa type only

Siva'pi (rabbit brush) stems for the Third Mesa wicker basketry are peeled and steeped in this dye. For this purpose, the mordanted dye is allowed to cool until nearly lukewarm, in a receptacle long enough to accommodate the length of the material (10-12 inches).

The stems are immersed in this, either loose or tied lightly in bundles, and the vessel is gently rocked at intervals, and the bundles turned to dye the material evenly.

Siva'pi dye may be considered as a "fairly fast" dye. It is permanent to washing but loses color when exposed to light over a long period — turns brown.

Smoking

For an intense shade of gold: while still damp, bundles of dyed basketry material may be placed in the smoker and smoked until the desired shade is attained, in about ½ hour or until material dries. It may be necessary to re-dip in dye several times during the smoking process. (See Chapter V.)

Stock Dye No. 1   RABBIT BRUSH
                       SIVA'PI YELLOW
                  siva'pi (Chrysothamnus sp.)
Use tall variety — flowers large and decidedly yellow.
2 double handfuls (80 grams) of blossoms. Add 8 cups (2
litres) of water, or sufficient to cover well. Bring to boil slowly.
Boil 1-2 hours gently and reduce to 6 cups (1½ litres) of dye.
Strain through a cotton cloth and squeeze out well.

Result: A clear, dark amber liquid. This liquid should be strained
off through a cloth and well squeezed out. The resulting liquid
or stock dye should now be replaced upon the stove and
ground or melted native alum added to the clear liquor, when
the dye will immediately turn an opaque, greenish-yellow.
After this has been boiled for a few minutes and slightly
cooled, it will be ready to receive the damp wool or cotton to
be dyed. The pan may then be set upon the stove and reheated, but not boiled. If an intense shade is desired, remove
and smoke while damp.

Stock Dye No. 2

1 double handful (40 grams) *siva'pi* blossoms. 3 cups (½ litre
stale urine. 3 cups (½ litre) water or enough to cover blossoms
well. Bring to a boil slowly. Boil 1 hour. Strain through cotton
cloth and squeeze out well.

Result: Dark brown liquid.

Stock Dye No. 3   RABBIT BRUSH
                        SIVA'PI YELLOW
                    siva'pi (Chrysothamnus sp.)

Use stems.

Break *siva'pi* stems and pack into 4-quart kettle. Cover with water, about 16 cups (4 litres). Boil slowly for 2 hours, adding water when necessary. Reduce liquid to 8 cups (2 litres). Strain through cloth.

Result: Pale, yellowish-green liquid.

Stock Dye No. 4

Use blossoms, tallest variety; flowers are long and pale, straw color; yellow blossom tip not prominent.

1 double handful (40 grams) *siva'pi* blossoms. 8 cups (2 litres) of water or sufficient to cover well. Bring to a boil slowly. Boil 1-2 hours gently and reduce to 6 cups (1½ litres). Strain through cloth — squeeze out.

Result: Clear, brownish-yellow liquid.

YELLOWS AND GOLDS
RABBIT BRUSH   *siva'pi (Chrysothamnus sp.)*

Use Stock Dye No. 1.

To dye wool: Wool should be placed damp in the warm mordanted dye bath and brought to a boil slowly and boiled gently for several hours, or until the desired shade is obtained. If a more intense shade is desired, remove the wool and smoke while still damp.

To dye cotton: Cotton, like most vegetable fibers, takes the dye best when soaked in the dye bath. It should be placed, damp, in the mordanted dye and brought slowly to a boil and boiled gently for a few minutes only. It should then be set aside and soaked for 12 hours.

Recipe No. 1   RABBIT BRUSH   For wool, cotton and basketry
SIVA'PI YELLOW
siva'pi (Chrysothamnus sp.)

Use Stock Dye No. 1.

Add to this liquid 1 double handful (100 ml.) of ground native alum. Liquid at once turns an opaque, greenish-yellow.

Material added: Into 6 cups (1½ litres) of dye, immerse 1 double handful (40 grams) of wool washed in yucca suds or cotton soaked in hot water.

Treatment in dye: Bring to a boil slowly and boil 1-2 hours.

After treatment: Remove material, wring slightly and dry. After drying, rinse thoroughly.

Result: Wool, good, brilliant yellow; cotton, good; basketry fibers, good.

Variation: For cotton, better results are obtained in most cases, by immersing in a hot dye bath, bringing to boil, then setting aside to soak for 12 hours.

Recipe No. 2   RABBIT BRUSH   For wool and cotton
SIVA'PI YELLOW
siva'pi (Chrysothamnus sp.)

Use Stock Dye No. 1 and Recipe No. 1.

Material added: Into 6 cups (1½ litres) of Stock Dye No. 1 immerse 1 double handful (40 grams) of wool washed in yucca suds or cotton soaked in hot water.

Treatment in dye: Bring to boil slowly and boil 1-2 hours.

After treatment: Remove material and wring slightly. Dry and rinse thoroughly.

Result: Wool, good, greenish-yellow; cotton, better results are obtained by immersing in hot dye bath, bringing to boil and then soaking for 12 hours, instead of boiling in dye.

(Maerz and Paul, 12-L-3, Pyrite Yellow R.)

Recipe No. 3   RABBIT BRUSH   For wool and cotton
                                SIVA'PI YELLOW
                          siva'pi (Chrysothamnus sp.)

Use Stock Dye No. 4.

Mordanting: Add to this liquid 1 double handful (100 ml.) of
  ground native alum. Liquid turns a light, opaque, yellowish-
  green.

Material added: Into 8 cups (2 litres) of dye, immerse 1 double
  handful (30-40 grams) of wool washed in yucca suds or
  cotton soaked in hot water.

Treatment in dye: Boil 2 to 3 hours.

After treatment: Remove, wring slightly and dry; then rinse
  thoroughly.

Result: Wool, a nice pale yellow; cotton, dull. Better results obtained on cotton immersed in hot dye, brought to boil and
  soaked 12 hours. Result: color similar.
  (Maerz and Paul, 11-L-2, Pyrethrum Yellow)

Recipe No. 4   RABBIT BRUSH   For wool and cotton
                                SIVA'PI YELLOW
                          siva'pi (Chrysothamnus sp.)

Use Stock Dye No. 4.

Mordanting: Add to this 1 double handful (100 ml.) of ground
  native alum. Liquid at once turns an opaque, brownish-yellow.

Material added: Into 6 cups (1½ litres) of dye immerse 1 double
  handful (40 grams) of wool washed in yucca suds or cotton
  soaked in hot water.

Treatment in dye: Bring to boil slowly and boil 1-2 hours.

After treatment: Remove material, wring slightly and dry. Rinse
  thoroughly.

Result: Wool, a fine, golden-green; cotton, color rather dull.

Soaking: Cotton brought to boil only and then soaked in dye for
  12 hours gives a much brighter shade.
  (Maerz and Paul, cotton; 11-K-3, Colonial Yellow)

Smoking: Smoking cotton and wool intensifies color slightly and
  renders material more permanent.

Recipe No. 5   RABBIT BRUSH   For wool
SIVA'PI YELLOW
siva'pi (Chrysothamnus sp.)
Use stems, tall variety.
Boil stems 2 hours in 8 cups (2 litres) water. Resulting liquid, pale greenish.
Mordanting: Add 40 grams of native alum. Resulting liquid light, opaque, yellow-green.
Material added: Wash wool in yucca; immerse and boil for 2 hours.
Result: Pale yellow, washes satisfactorily.

Recipe No. 6   RABBIT BRUSH   For wool and cotton
SIVA'PI YELLOW
siva'pi (Chrysothamnus sp.)
Use blossoms; large blossoms with yellow tip in end of blossom; possibly the tallest variety.
Put 2 double handfuls blossoms in 8 cups (2 litres) water. Boil 2 hours. Strain liquid which is dull, yellowish-brown.
Mordanting: Add 40 grams native alum; turns opaque, yellow-brown.
Material added: Put in wool washed in yucca and boil 2 hours. Dry and wash wool. Boil cotton in water, immerse in hot dye and soak for 4 hours.
Result: Wool, a fine greenish, canary yellow; cotton, bright yellow.

Recipe No. 7   RABBIT BRUSH   For wool and cotton
SIVA'PI YELLOW
siva'pi (Chrysothamnus sp.)
Smoking: Smoking dyed cotton and wool slightly intensifies color and renders shades more permanent. Place, while damp, in a smoker and smoke until material dries or the desired color is obtained. Remove and rinse thoroughly in lukewarm water.
Result: Wool, a good, brilliant yellow; cotton, similar to wool.

Recipe No. 8   RABBIT BRUSH   For wool and cotton
                     SIVA'PI YELLOW
                   siva'pi (Chrysothamnus sp.)

Siva'pi blossoms — they are the largest type of blossoms and a very pale color. The blossom tip is not as bright yellow as the other varieties. Put 2 double handfuls blossoms in ¾ cup (200 ml.) of water. Boil 4 hours and strain. This produces a pale brownish liquid.

Mordanting: Add 40 grams native alum. Liquid turns opaque, greenish-yellow.

Material added: Wash Navajo wool in yucca and rinse. Immerse in dye. It assumes a pale canary color. Boil 2 hours. Soak cotton in dye; do not boil.

Result: A fine, canary yellow. Smoking intensifies color. Cotton rather dull.

YELLOWS AND GOLDS
na'palnga or Golden Rod *(Solidago* sp.)

Habitat, character and properties as a dye

There are many species of golden rod, large and small, growing at different altitudes and under many conditions all over the United States.

It bears heads of small composite flowers of a golden color, which produce a rich dye. This dye is similar in character and in its reactions to the *siva'pi* yellow dyes.

This dye was used by early American (white) dyers and weavers, and there is also a possibility that it was used by the Hopi, but this cannot be stated positively.

Golden rod makes an excellent dye for cotton, wool and basketry material. (For basketry, see recipe for *siva'pi* yellows.)

Stock Dye No. 1   GOLDENROD
YELLOWS AND GOLDS
na'palnga (Solidago sp.)

Use blossoms.

2 double handfuls (30 grams) of blossoms to 8 cups (2 litres) of water, or sufficient to cover well. Bring to boil slowly. Boil gently 1-2 hours and reduce to 6 cups (1½ litres). Strain through cotton cloth. Squeeze out well.

Result: Clear, golden-brown liquid.

Recipe No. 1   GOLDENROD   For wool and cotton
                        YELLOWS AND GOLDS
                        na'palnga (Solidago sp.)

Use Stock Dye No. 1.

Mordanting: Add to this liquid 1 double handful of ground native
    alum. Liquid at once turns an opaque, greenish-yellow.

Material added: Into 6 cups (1½ litres) of dye, immerse 1 double
    handful (40 grams) of wool washed in yucca suds or cotton
    soaked in hot water.

Treatment in dye: Bring to boil slowly and simmer gently 1-2 hours.

After treatment: Remove material, wring slightly and dry; then
    rinse thoroughly.

Result: Wool and cotton, a very brilliant, canary yellow. These
    shades are more intense than any other yellows. Turns slightly
    more reddish in time, but is fast.

    (Maerz and Paul, 11-L-1, Chartreuse)

Recipe No. 2   GOLDENROD   For wool and cotton
                        YELLOWS AND GOLDS
                        na'palnga (Solidago sp.)

Use Stock Dye No. 1 and Recipe No. 1.

When material has been removed from dye, place in boiling
soapy water (Ivory Flakes) and simmer a few minutes.

After treatment: Remove, rinse, wring slightly and dry.

Result: A very rich, deep, gold color.

    (Maerz and Paul, 11-L-5, Lime Yellow)

Stock Dye No. 1

MINERAL YELLOW

Take 1 large double handful of Mancos Shale containing limonite found near Polacca, and cover with 4 cups (1 litre) of water. Crush lumps of earth with fingers and stir the mass every few minutes, then let it settle. A clear liquid will rise to the top as the earth settles and will gradually turn a deep, clear, claret-red color. Allow this to stand overnight. Decant and use as it is, or put through filter paper.

Result: A perfectly clear claret-red liquid. No odor nor reaction to changes in temperature. Sand left after settling is a very fine, gray material.

Recipe No. 1   For wool
MINERAL YELLOW
Use Stock Dye No. 1.

Preparation of material: Take wool that has been washed in yucca suds and rinse.

Treatment in dye: Place in warm dye and stand aside to soak. Soak 24 hours.

After treatment: Remove, wring slightly and dry. Rinse thoroughly.

Result: A good yellow-ochre color.

Washing test: Very fast.

APRICOTS AND GOLDS
saya'vi or Canaigre *(Rumex hymenosepalus)*

Habitat, character and properties as a dye

The desert dock grows in the beds of sandy washes and on flats and it is occasionally cultivated by certain tribes. It has a long carrot-like root. This is gathered and used to produce a fine gold or orange-apricot dye. The root may be used while fresh, or, dried and stored. It yields an abundance of rich brown dye which seems equally effective on wool or cotton.

Note: Also used by Navajo (Bryan and Young, 1940, p. 28).

Basketry

It is said to be a good dye for basketry materials also. The writer has not experimented with these fibers, but recommends doing so.

Stock Dye No. 1   CANAIGRE
APRICOTS AND GOLDS
saya'vi (Rumex hymenosepalus)

Take the long carrot-like root of the desert dock and brush off sand. Put about 6 of these roots into a large kettle and cover with cold water; let them soak overnight. In the morning they will be soft and must be carefully peeled; do not remove more of the skin than necessary. Cut them up into small pieces and replace in the water in which they have soaked overnight. Put on the stove and bring to boil slowly. Boil gently several hours. Remove and strain through a cloth and squeeze out liquor.

Result: A clear, dark brown liquor.

Recipe No. 1   **CANAIGRE**   For wool and cotton

APRICOTS AND GOLDS

saya'vi (Rumex hymenosepalus)

Use Stock Dye No. 1.

Mordanting: This dye is a "natural dye" and contains within itself both dye and mordant, probably tannin. Therefore, it needs no additional mordanting.

Material added: To 6 cups (1½ litres) of this dye add 1 double handful (30-40 grams) of wool washed in yucca suds and rinsed or cotton soaked in hot water.

Treatment in dye: Immerse in dye, bring to boil slowly and boil 1-2 hours.

After treatment: Remove, wring slightly and dry, then rinse thoroughly.

Result: A fine, old gold.

Washing test: Very fast.

(Maerz and Paul, 13-L-7, Tinsel Deep Stone)

Variation: When alum is added to this dye, a more brilliant yellow results.

(Maerz and Paul, 12-L-5, Sulphin Yellow)

Recipe No. 2   **CANAIGRE**   For wool and cotton

APRICOT

saya'vi (Rumex hymenosepalus)

Use Stock Dye No. 1 and Recipe No. 1.

After treatment: When material has been removed from dye and wrung slightly, place it while damp in warm stale urine. Work it in the urine for about 10 minutes. Remove and rinse thoroughly several times in hot water and dry in the sun.

Result: A fine shade of apricot.

(Maerz and Paul, 12-A-11, Maya)

Washing test: Very fast.

Smoked: Similar results may be obtained by smoking the material when removed from the dye bath. This color is not as pink as when not smoked.

CHAPTER IX

Blues

Indigo blue — natural or vegetable indigo

THE CULTIVATION AND THE USE of indigo is very ancient both in India, the East Indies, in Central America and Mexico.

Indigo is grown principally in India and Indonesia today where it has been used for centuries for the dyeing of cotton fabrics and other vegetable fibers.

From prehistoric times it was grown and used as a textile dye in Central America. There is strong evidence that it was a valuable article of trade, which, traveling from tribe to tribe through Mexico, finally reached our own prehistoric peoples of the southwestern United States.

It is certain that up to fifty years ago, impure lump indigo was still traded into the pueblos of the Rio Grande Valley. With the discovery of synthetic indigo, commercial cultivation of the plant ceased in Central America and Mexico and the supply from this ancient source was cut off.

Indigo produces the finest shades of blue (slightly greenish) on cotton, wool and other vegetable and animal fibers. It is absolutely permanent.

There are many methods of dyeing with indigo. One of the oldest of these, is the Cold Indigo Vat prepared with stale urine. This has long been in use in many parts of the world. This method is still used today by the Hopi, Navajo and other Pueblo peoples of the Southwest.*

Of all the dyes used by the Hopi, indigo is the most precious to him. It is the sacred color of the sky. The Hopi name, *saqwa*, is

* Indigo is not mentioned by Bryan and Young, 1940, for the Navajo.

used to mean blue, of the sky, the precious turquoise, and the blue of flowers, birds and butterflies. Next to turquoise, it is the most precious thing that he might possess.

Synthetic indigo can be purchased from Du Pont but it is not recommended for the Hopi because it requires the use of sodium hydroxide which is dangerous to have around a home with children running about. It does not require the use of urine as a reducing agent because other chemicals are used for reduction. It is easy to use but is not recommended for a household industry.

Recipe No. 1   For wool, cotton and basketry

INDIGO BLUE
(lump indigo*)

Preparation of urine — collect human urine in a large pottery storage jar, keeping the top carefully sealed. Allow to stand in a warm room for some days or until it gives off a strong odor of ammonia. It is now ready for use. 2 gallons of stale urine in 4 gallon jar. About 1 large double handful (270 grams) of indigo lumps. Tie indigo in cloth, dip in liquid and beat out color against the side of the jar as it dissolves. Then allow indigo sack to remain in liquid. Stand this jar overnight in a warm room, either covered with a close top or with cloth tied tightly over the top.

Preparation of material: Next day take 2 hanks of spun yarn, cotton or wool, or about 2 pounds that has been thoroughly washed in yucca suds before spinning.

Material added: Wet this thoroughly in cold water. If wool soak, if cotton wring out gently and place in the indigo, which now appears to be covered with a greenish scum.

Treatment in dye: Stir down and thoroughly soak yarn in dye by manipulation with sticks. Prepare 6 small sticks just the width of the jar top and wedge them in on top of the floating yarn, thus keeping the material below the surface of the dye. Let this stand for 4 days — open the jar each day and thoroughly "handle" the·wool with a pair of sticks. If this is not done, the wool will turn greenish wherever the air touches it and will not take the dye evenly.

After treatment: On the fourth day, remove the wool and wring it out lightly. The wool will appear green when first exposed to the air. It should be hung at once in the open air where oxidation will take place and it will shortly turn a fine, rich, dark blue. Allow it to dry thoroughly then rinse in a succession of warm waters until wool ceases to yield color, when it should again be hung in the air and dried.

Cotton as well as Third Mesa basketry material may be dyed in the same manner and results are equally good.

* Lump indigo can be purchased through the Museum of Northern Arizona, Flagstaff, Arizona.

Result: Wool and cotton both a fine, deep blue. For a light, bright blue, two days soaking will be found sufficient.

Washing test: Fast.

Light test: Fast.

(Maerz and Paul, wool, 39-A-12; cotton, 38-H-6, Harbor Blue)

BLUES
tupénmori or Blue Kidney Bean *(Phaseolus vulgaris)*

Habitat, character and properties as a dye

This bean is said to be of a very ancient type. It is cultivated today by the Hopi. It is valued particularly as a source of blue dye.

It is a solid blue-black bean of the kidney type with a powdery bloom on the surface, ends are square to rounded and the size is variable, usually quite small.

Like sunflower seed and corn, the bean has a starchy interior and the dye is in the outer skin of the shell. Therefore, care must be taken not to allow this bean to boil *after the skin has cracked open,* or the color of the dye will be spoiled by the starchy interior.

This bean produces a blue dye effective on cotton and on wicker basketry fibers. It cannot be used on wool.

Colors range from blues to purple-blues.

Stock Dye No. 1 **BLUE KIDNEY BEAN** For cotton and basketry
BLUES
tupénmori (Phaseolus vulgaris)

3 double handfuls (450 ml.) of beans. 10 cups (2½ litres) of water. Bring to boil slowly. Boil gently for 20 minutes to ½ hour, or until skin of beans begins to crack open. Strain through cloth.

Result: Dirty, brownish-blue liquid.

Recipe No. 1   BLUE KIDNEY BEAN   For cotton and basketry
                     PURPLE-BLUE
                     tupénmori (Phaseolus vulgaris)

Use Stock Dye No. 1.

Mordanting: Add to the liquid stock dye 1 small double handful
(100 ml.) of ground native alum. Liquid instantly turns an
intense, deep purple. Boil down to 6 cups (1½ litres) of dye.

Material added: To 6 cups (1½ litres) of this dye add 1 double
handful (30-40 grams) of cotton or cotton yarn which has been
soaked 24-48 hours in a preparation of ground copper carbonate
and water. (See Purple Corn Dye, Recipe No. 6.) Remove and
press out water lightly.

Treatment in dye: Immerse in hot dye bath and soak several hours,
or until a good shade is procured.

After treatment: Remove and dry without wringing. Rinse thoroughly and press out lightly.

Result: A fine, clear, purple-blue.

(Maerz and Paul, 43-A-5)

Recipe No. 2   BLUE KIDNEY BEAN   For cotton and basketry
                BLUE-PURPLE
                tupénmori (Phaseolus vulgaris)

Use Stock Dye No. 1 and Recipe No. 1.

Preparation of material: Substitute cotton washed in Lux or Ivory
soap, rinse, then soak.

Treatment in dye: Immerse in dye and soak several hours.

After treatment: Remove, without wringing. Rinse thoroughly *after
drying* and re-dry.

Result: Good, deep blue-purple. Dulled by rinsing.

Recipe No. 3   BLUE KIDNEY BEAN   For cotton and basketry
                 PURPLE-BLUE
                 tupénmori (Phaseolus vulgaris)

Use Stock Dye No. 1 and Recipe No. 1.

Preparation of material: Substitute spun cotton boiled and soaked in plain water, squeeze out lightly and immerse in dye.

Treatment in dye: Soak several hours.

After treatment: Remove from dye. Dry without wringing. Rinse thoroughly after drying and re-dry.

Result: Color similar to cotton soaked in copper carbonate, a fine, clear, purple-blue. This is good for basketry material also. (Maerz and Paul, 43-B-7, Ontario Violet)

BLUE KIDNEY BEAN   For basketry
BLUES

tupénmori (Phaseolus vulgaris)

This dye is a good basketry dye, especially effective on the peeled stems of the rabbit brush, *(siva'pi)*, used in wicker basketry. Any of the recipes given may be used, with the possible exception of Recipe No. 1.

Dyeing

For this purpose, the mordanted dye is allowed to cool until nearly lukewarm, in a receptacle long enough to accommodate the length of the material (10-12 inches).

The stems are immersed in this, either loose or tied lightly in bundles, and the bundles are turned so that the material will be evenly dyed.

Smoking

For strong shades of blue:

While still damp, bundles of dyed basketry material should be placed in the smoker and smoked until the desired shade is obtained. It may be necessary to re-dip in dye several times during the smoking process. (See Chapter V.)

Bean Blue Dip

Dip basketry material in Bean Blue Dye. Have wet sand ready on a canvas and put the blue dyed basketry material in the sand and work it about.

Result: a brilliant blue.

CHAPTER X

Blues and Purples, Carmine Reds, Maroons

Stock Dye No. 1

'a:'qaw'u or Sunflower Seed *(Helianthus* sp.)

Sunflower seed — 2 double handfuls (300 ml.). Water — 8 cups (2 litres). Bring to boil slowly. Boil gently not more than ½ hour, or until seeds split open. Strain through cloth.

Result: Deep maroon liquid.

Recipe No. 1   SUNFLOWER SEED   For wool and cotton
PURPLE
'a:'qaw'u *(Helianthus* sp.)

Use Stock Dye No. 1.

Mordanting: Add to this liquid 1 small double handful (100 ml.) of ground native alum. Dye turns a deep, royal purple.

Material added: To 6 cups (1½ litres) of this dye, add 1 double handful (40 grams) of wool washed in yucca suds and rinsed or cotton soaked in hot water.

Treatment in dye: Immerse in dye. Bring to boil slowly. Boil gently about ½ hour and remove from fire.

After treatment: Allow material to soak in dye for 24 hours. Remove material, wring slightly, dry and rinse thoroughly after drying.

Result: Wool, a dull, dark lavender; cotton, a fine, deep purple.

Washing test: Wool not fast.

Light test: Cotton turns bluish.

(Maerz and Paul, wool, 47-C-7; cotton, 47-E-8)

57

Recipe No. 2   SUNFLOWER SEED   For wool
                           BLUE
                 'a:'qaw'u (Helianthus sp.)

Use Stock Dye No. 1.

Mordanting: Add to this liquid 1 small double handful (100 ml.) of ground native alum. Dye turns a deep, royal purple.

Material added: To 6 cups (1½ litres) of this dye, add 1 double handful (40 grams) of wool which has been washed and boiled ½ hour in Lux or Ivory soap and rinsed.

Treatment in dye: Immerse in dye and bring to boil slowly. Boil gently 1-2 hours.

After treatment: Remove, wring slightly, and dry; rinse thoroughly.

Result: Wool, a good blue.

Washing test: Not fast to soap.

                 SUNFLOWER SEED   For basketry material
                 BLUES AND PURPLES
                 'a:'qaw'u (Helianthus sp.)

These recipes are effective on wicker basketry (peeled stems of *siva'pi* or rabbit brush). Fine blues and purples can be produced.

Dyeing

The mordanted dye is allowed to cool until nearly lukewarm, in a receptacle long and deep enough to accommodate the length of the material (10-12 inches). The stems are immersed in this dye bath either loose or tied lightly in bundles. The vessel is gently agitated at intervals and the bundles turned, so that the dye will take evenly on the material.

Smoking

The smoking of sunflower seed blues and red-purples, causes the blues to darken and dull and the red-purples to turn a cold blue. If this is desired, while still damp, bundles of dyed basketry material can be placed in the smoker and smoked until the desired shade is obtained. (See Chapter V.)

koko'ma or PURPLE CORN
(Zea mays amylacea)

History

The Hopi Indians believe this corn to be one of the oldest original types of corn which they possess.

Formerly a Hopi used great care in planting his corn of different colors in separate plots, not because he realized that the varieties would cross, but from some obscure feeling that each of the sacred colors should have its own ground.

The main types of corn recognized by the Hopi are those colors which stand for the "six directions" of the Hopi compass. These read from left to right, and are represented on the sacred altars thus:

Northeast — yellow corn
Northwest — blue corn
Southwest — red corn
Southeast — white corn
Upward — purple corn
Downward — sweet or flint corn

With the exception of the sweet and flint corns, the other color varieties are all flour corns. The Hopi claim that all these varieties of corn are their own from ancient times. Other varieties of lesser importance recognized, are popcorn, blue spotted corn, gray-blue corn and lavender corn. The people realize today that all varieties of corn cross, and that this accounts for the many mixtures of flint, dent and flour corns and their myriad color varieties.

Its character — properties as a dye

The coloring matter extracted from *koko'ma* or purple corn is used today for a number of purposes by the Hopi. A young boy's first ceremonial kilt of hand spun cotton is dyed a soft lavender-blue in this dye. This kilt is not boiled in the dye but soaked.

Corn dye is used as a textile dye for both cotton and wool and also for basketry material on Third Mesa. As a paint with a base of white clay, it is used on ceremonial wooden objects and as a body paint. It seems most probable that at one time *koko'ma* dye was more extensively used for cotton textiles and later possibly for wool, but at present only a faint trace of its former uses upon textiles can be discovered.

Proceeding with this theory, and because actual recipes for

further uses of this dye may be unearthed at any time, the writer has made a series of experiments, the results of which are given under the recipes for *koko'ma* dyes. In carrying out these experiments both the native mordants derived from local plants and minerals, and the common modern soaps and household cleaners have been used. No chemicals to which the Indian would not have had access, either in ancient or in modern times, have been introduced.

The best type of this corn to use as a dye is the deep purple or almost black type. The cob must also be purple for the best results. The purple cob is also used for dye and produces a lighter shade. The dyes produced from this corn are either a deep, royal purple or carmine-red, depending upon the mordanting. If the corn is white, a strong dye cannot be made from the kernels.

Two main colors may be derived from the kernels of the purple corn and from these a great variety of shades may be produced by variations in handling and the use of the mordants.

Stock Dye No. 1

The shelled purple corn is placed in an enamel vessel and well covered with cold water. This is brought slowly to a boil and allowed to boil gently not longer than ½ hour. As it begins to heat, a purple-red color is given off. This deepens with boiling to a fine, clear, carmine-red.

This dye is very sensitive to changes of temperature and extremely tricky, especially before the mordant has been added. It should be boiled gently for not more than ½ hour, or *until the grains begin to crack open*, when it must be removed at once and the liquor strained off through a fine sieve or cloth. The result is a fine, clear, deep carmine-red liquor.

If the corn is allowed to boil too long after the grains have cracked, the dye rapidly turns brownish. If this dye is chilled and reheated or boiled at a high temperature, it will also lose color. Therefore, when the liquor has been strained off, it should be kept warm and used as soon as possible.

This dye stock may now be treated in four ways:

Method 1. It may have the concentrated liquor of sumac berries added to it. This causes the dye to brighten in color.

Method 2. Ground native alum may be added. This causes the carmine dye to turn at once, a deep, fine purple. But, if this dye is subjected to much heat, or to boiling more than five or ten minutes, it will gradually revert toward the red.

Method 3. The stock dye may have some sumac berry liquor added to it, and in a few minutes a small amount of ground native alum. In this case the alum, added after the sumac berry liquor, only brightens the dye and does not cause it to turn purple. After boiling this dye for more than ½ hour, it may lose brilliancy. The addition of more sumac berry liquor will revive it. After this, it would seem that the dye has reached an equilibrium and will now stand boiling for any length of time without changing color. It will stand for days and can be reheated without undergoing any noticeable change.

Method 4. The stock dye may have ground native alum added to it, as in method 2, when it turns a deep purple .This dye may then be boiled for several hours, when it gradually loses the purple color and reverts to a carmine-red. In this state it seems stable and no longer sensitive to temperature changes. Unwashed wool and cotton, mordanted in weak lye water, and dyed in this dye, becomes a fine, carmine-pink. This color is fast to rinsing in warm water and even to soap, but will not stand high temperatures which cause it to lose color and turn gray-blue.

Summary of Various Methods

Method 1. Both wool and cotton can be dyed with this method; wool, a good maroon that is fairly fast and cotton a good, carmine-pink, either by boiling or, preferably, by soaking. However, this color is not fast on cotton, either to washing or to light. Even rinsing causes it to turn bluish.

Method 2. Both wool and cotton can be dyed by this method and good shades of purple, lavender, and slate blue can be produced, depending upon the method of washing and preparing the wool and cotton, (see recipes). Though several of these shades are in the "fairly fast" class, they all have a tendency to turn toward blue when washed and to lose color from prolonged exposure to light.

Method 3. Both wool and cotton can be dyed by this method and the beautiful shades of raspberry-red and maroon produced on wool are the most permanent to washing, of this group, especially when they are smoked after dyeing. Prolonged exposure to light turns them brownish, although fine shades of pink, to lustrous maroon, can be produced on cotton, they are not fast to washing, as they at once turn blue, even when rinsed. The same is the case when material is smoked. Light also fades them badly.

Method 4. Both wool and cotton can be dyed by this method and fine shades of carmine-pink produced. These are quite fast to rinsing and even to washing with soap and warm water, but will not stand high temperatures. They turn a dirty bluish color. The same is the case when material is smoked.

Conclusions: While corn dye can be made to produce many fine soft shades on cotton, wool and basketry, ranging through purples and slate blues to carmine-reds, maroons, browns and tans, none of these can be considered in the permanent class. In both washing and light tests they lose color.

PURPLE CORN   For basketry
CARMINE AND RED-BROWN
koko'ma (Zea mays amylacea)

Third Mesa wicker basketry material can be dyed with any of the following methods.

The dye is placed in a container of sufficient length to accommodate the material. The *siva'pi* (rabbit brush) stems are then immersed in the lukewarm mordanted dye, either loose or in bundles, and soaked.

The vessel is rocked at intervals and the bundles turned, so that the material will dye evenly.

Occasionally it is carefully reheated during the process.

The carmine and red-brown shades from this dye are not smoked, as it causes them to change color.

Stock Dye No. 1   PURPLE CORN
                      CARMINE
          koko'ma (Zea mays amylacea)

Corn — 3 double handfuls (450 grams). Water — 10 cups (2½ litres). Bring to boil slowly. Boil gently ¾ hour or until kernels begin to crack open. Strain through cloth.

Result: Deep, carmine-red liquid.

Stock Dye No. 2   PURPLE CORN
            KOKO'MA BROWN
        koko'ma (Zea mays amylacea)

Break corncobs that are a deep, red-purple in small sections and half fill a 6-quart kettle. Cover with 16 cups (4 litres) of water. Bring to boil slowly. Boil gently for 1-2 hours. Boil down to ½ quantity. Strain through cloth.

Result: Deep, carmine-red liquid (not quite as intense as that from corn kernels).

Stock Dye No. 3   PURPLE CORN
            KOKO'MA RED
        koko'ma (Zea mays amylacea)

Corn — 5 double handfuls (750 grams). Water — 16 cups (4 litres). Bring to boil slowly. Boil gently ¾ hour or until kernels begin to crack open. Strain through cloth.

Result: Deep, carmine-red liquid.

Recipe No. 1   PURPLE CORN   For wool and cotton
                              KOKO'MA PURPLE
                          koko'ma (Zea mays amylacea)

Use Stock Dye No. 1.

Mordanting: dye and mordant one process. Add to this, 1 small
    double handful (100 grams) of ground native alum. Liquid
    at once turns deep purple. Boil down to 6 cups (1½ litres).

Material added: To about 6 cups (1½ litres) of this dye add 1
    double handful (30-40 grams) of wool washed with a neutral
    soap or cotton boiled in plain water.

Treatment in dye: Immerse in dye, bring to boiling point slowly and
    boil 15-20 minutes. Remove from fire.

After treatment: Set aside and soak for 48 hours. Remove from dye,
    wring lightly and dry, then rinse thoroughly after drying.

Result: Wool, deep purple; cotton, deep purple.

Washing test: Wool, fairly fast to rinsing; cotton, same.

Light test: Does not fade.

    (Maerz and Paul, 46-F-6)

Test No. 1 (alkali)

Use Stock Dye No. 1 and Recipe No. 1.

Preparation of material: Substitute wool washed and boiled in Lux
    soap for ½ hour.

After treatment: Set aside and soak for 24 hours, or 48 hours, if
    purple is desired.

Result: Wool, good lavender; smoked, slightly darker; cotton, same.

Washing test: Fairly fast, slightly lighter. More bluish, good.

Test No. 2 (alkali acid)

Use Stock Dye No. 1 and Recipe No. 1.

Preparation of material: Wool washed in Lux soap and then boiled
    in sumac berry liquid before dyeing.

Result: Saddens* purple toward brown.

----

* Sadden — make dark or dull.

Recipe No. 2   PURPLE CORN   For wool and cotton
                         KOKO'MA PURPLE
                   koko'ma (Zea mays amylacea)
Use Stock Dye No. 1 and Recipe No. 1.

Preparation of material: Use wool washed in yucca suds and rinsed;
   weak alkali.

Treatment in dye: Immerse in dye. Boil ½ hour.

After treatment: Remove from stove, set aside and soak 24 hours.

Result: Wool, fair lavender; cotton, fine purple.

Washing test: Wool, fairly fast, paler, more bluish; cotton, not fast,
   turns blue.

   (Maerz and Paul, 45-D-8, 46-H-9, 47-E-7)

Recipe No. 3   PURPLE CORN   For wool and cotton
                         KOKO'MA PURPLE
                   koko'ma (Zea mays amylacea)
Use Stock Dye No. 1 and Recipe No. 1.

Preparation of material: Use carefully selected wool, with the dirt
   well shaken out. Soak in warm lye water for ½ hour (alkalizer).
   Wring slightly and immerse in dye. Do not wash.

Result: Wool, a fine, deep purple; cotton, a fine, deep, reddish-
   purple.

Washing test: Wool, fast — turns slightly bluish; cotton, fast — loses
   reddish tinge.

   (Maerz and Paul, wool, 47-E-8; cotton, 46-K-8)

Recipe No. 4   PURPLE CORN   For wool
                                KOKO'MA PURPLE
                          koko'ma (Zea mays amylacea)

Use Stock Dye No. 1.

Wool — 2 lots

Mordanting: Lot No. 1, washed in yucca suds and rinsed. (Cleanser
and mordant in one.)

Lot No. 2, washed in Lux soap and rinsed. (Weak alkaline
dyes.)

Treatment in dye: Immerse these two lots of wool into two separate
hot dye baths and bring slowly to boil. Boil gently for 15
minutes.

After treatment: Remove dye containers from stove and allow wool
to remain in dye bath for 24 hours. Remove, press out surplus
dye, shake out and dry.

Result: Brilliant purple.

Washing test: Wool, fairly fast to rinsing in plain water.

Recipe No. 5   PURPLE CORN   For wool and cotton
                           KOKO'MA PURPLE
                     koko'ma (Zea mays amylacea)

Use Stock Dye No. 1.

Mordanting (before dyeing): Take 1 small handful (100 grams) of
    ground native alum and dissolve in about 2 litres of warm
    water.

Material added: Place 1 double handful (30-40 grams) spun yarn
    or loose wool or cotton in warm alum water, bring to boil
    slowly and boil gently about 15 or 20 minutes. Remove the
    mordanted yarn, wring lightly and place at once in warm dye
    bath, about 6 cups (1½ litres).

The dye bath: Bring to boil and boil gently for about ½ hour. Stir
    and turn the yarn about in the dye bath.

After treatment: Remove from fire, press out surplus dye, shake
    out material and dry, then rinse thoroughly.

Result: Wool, a brilliant purple; cotton, same.

Washing test: Neither wool nor cotton lose color when rinsed in
    plain water. (Washed with Ivory soap, turns slightly bluish.)
    (Maerz and Paul, 44-B-6)

Recipe No. 6   PURPLE CORN   For cotton
CLOUD LAVENDER, CEREMONIAL DYE
koko'ma (Zea mays amylacea)

Use Stock Dye No. 1.

Mordanting: Add to this 1 small double handful (100 grams) of ground native alum. Liquid at once turns deep purple. Allow this dye, about 8 cups (2 litres) to heat slowly but do not bring to boil.

Preparation of material: Grind copper carbonate to powder on stone mortar; 1 double handful (75 ml.) to about 1½ gallons of water. Stand aside in jar. Soak cotton ceremonial kilt or spun cotton for 2-4 days in this mixture. Remove, dry and shake out.

Treatment in dye: Rinse material and place wet in 8 cups (2 litres) of dye and soak ½ hour or until cotton assumes desired shade. Cotton takes deep purple after 1 hour soaking.

After treatment: Remove, wring slightly and dry. Rinse thoroughly.

Result: Cotton, fine lavender.

Washing test: Not fast. Washed with soap turns light blue.

Test No. 1

Use Stock Dye No. 1 and Recipe No. 6.

Preparation of material: Substitute wool or cotton that has been washed in Lux soap and rinsed and then boiled ½ hour in alum water.

Treatment in dye: Immerse in dye, bring to boiling point slowly and boil 1 hour.

Result: Wool, a good, dark purple; cotton, same.

Washing test: Wool turns slightly bluish; cotton turns more purple.

Test No. 2

Use Stock Dye No. 1 and Recipe No. 6.

Material added: Substitute wool or cotton washed in Lux soap and rinsed.

Treatment in dye: Soak in dye 48 hours.

Result: Wool, a good, bright purple; cotton, same.

Washing test: Wool and cotton, not fast, lose color.

Recipe No. 7   PURPLE CORN   For wool, cotton and basketry
KOKO'MA CARMINE-PINK
koko'ma (Zea mays amylacea)

Use Stock Dye No. 1 or No. 3.

Mordanting: Add to this, 1 small double handful (100 ml.) of ground native alum. Liquid at once turns deep purple (alkaline). Now boil this gently for 1-2 hours and it will gradually lose its purple color and turn back toward the original carmine-red color (acid). Boil down to about 1/3 quantity of liquid or until the dye thickens slightly and becomes a very rich carmine color (acid). Now add enough warm water to bring the quantity up to 6 cups (1½ litres).

Material added: To this dye add 1 double handful (30-40 grams) of wool or cotton washed in yucca suds and soaked for ½ hour and then rinsed.

Treatment in dye: Immerse in dye, bring to boiling point slowly and boil gently for 1 hour.

After treatment: Set aside and soak overnight. Remove from dye, wring slightly and dry. Rinse thoroughly after drying.

Result: Wool, a fine, carmine-pink; cotton, the same. (The addition of an alkali to the purple corn turns it a blue-purple; while acid turns it a carmine-red.)

Recipe No. 8   PURPLE CORN   For cotton
                          KOKO'MA CARMINE-PINK
                          koko'ma (Zea mays amylacea)

Use Stock Dye No. 1 (acid dye).

Mordanting: Take 1 handful (20-25 grams) of sumac berries to 1-1/3 cups (300 ml.) of water and boil berries ½ hour, or they may be soaked 24 hours. Strain berries through cloth and squeeze out juice. Replace on fire and boil down to 6 cups (1½ litres).

Material added: Take cotton yarn or loose cotton and soak 24 hours in sumac berry acid, dry, then rinse.

Treatment in dye: Immerse cotton in bath of (acid) carmine dye (Stock Dye No. 1). Soak 3 or 4 hours.

After treatment: Remove, press out extra dye. Shake out yarn and dry; rinse in water to which has been added ½ cup of sumac berry acid (water may be slightly alkaline). Remove, shake out and dry.

Result: A fine, carmine-pink.

Test: Permanent to rinsing.

Recipe No. 9   PURPLE CORN   For wool and cotton
                          KOKO'MA CARMINE-RED
                          koko'ma (Zea mays amylacea)

Use Stock Dye No. 1 or No. 3 (acid dye).

Mordanting: Bring to boil and boil gently for 15 minutes. Now add enough water to bring the quantity up to 6 cups (1½ litres).

Material added: To this dye add 1 double handful (30-40 grams) of wool or cotton soaked in sumac berry acid. Wool washed in a neutral soap and rinsed. Cotton soaked in plain warm water (non-alkaline).

Treatment in dye: Immerse in dye and bring to boiling point slowly. Boil about 15 minutes. If dye turns dull, add more sumac berry acid.

After treatment: Set aside and soak overnight. Remove from dye, wring lightly and dry. Rinse in cold water after drying.

Result: Wool a fine, carmine-red.

Recipe No. 10   PURPLE CORN   For cotton
                      KOKO'MA RASPBERRY-RED
                        koko'ma (Zea mays amylacea)

Preparation of material: Take cotton yarn or loose cotton, about 1
    double handful (10 grams) and soak 24 hours in sumac berry
    acid, dry and then rinse. Prepare a solution of cream of tar-
    tar; 500 grams cream of tartar in water. Now immerse cotton
    in solution of cream of tartar and allow to soak ½ hour. Remove
    and press out extra liquid.

Material added: Immerse in carmine dye bath and soak 3 or 4
    hours.

After treatment: Remove, press out dye and dry.

Result: Fine, deep, raspberry-red.

Remarks: If washed in alkaline water, will turn bluish.

Recipe No. 11   PURPLE CORN   For wool and cotton
                 KOKO'MA RASPBERRY-RED
                 koko'ma (Zea mays amylacea)

Use Stock Dye No. 3.

Mordanting: Replace on fire and boil down slowly to ½ quantity of liquid. Now add ¾ cup (200 ml.) of sumac berry liquid. Add 1 handful (25 ml.) of ground native alum. Alum added to carmine dye after addition of sumac acid does not turn carmine dye purple. Boil ½ hour and add second ¾ cup (200 ml.) of berry liquid. Acid and alkali maintain a balance and dye remains stable. Color unchanged by boiling for any length of time. Not affected by cooling and reheating.

Material added: To 6 cups (1½ litres) of this dye add 1 double handful (30-40 grams) of wool or cotton washed in yucca suds then boiled ½ hour in alum water and rinsed.

Treatment in dye: Bring to boiling point slowly and boil 2 hours; or soak in dye overnight and boil for 1 hour.

After treatment: Remove from dye, wring lightly and dry. Rinse thoroughly.

Result: Wool, deep carmine or raspberry-red; cotton, fine pink.

Washing test: Wool, fairly fast, slightly more brownish; cotton, turns bluish.

Test No. 1.

Cotton and wool unwashed and soaked in liquid sheep manure, boiled in above dye, fine, deep, raspberry-red.

Test No. 2.

Cotton and wool smoked after dyeing, intensifies color.

Recipe No. 12   PURPLE CORN   For wool and cotton
                       KOKO'MA MAROON
                    koko'ma (Zea mays amylacea)
Use Stock Dye No. 1.

Mordanting: Add to this, ½ cup (150 ml.) of liquid from sumac
   berries, produced by boiling berries ½ hour or soaking 24
   hours; 1 handful (20-25 grams) of berries in 1-1/3 cups (300
   ml.) of water. Strain berries through cloth and squeeze out
   juice. Replace on fire. Boil down to about 8 cups (2 litres).

Material added: To 8 cups (2 litres) of this dye add 1 double
   handful (30-40 grams) of wool or cotton washed or soaked
   in yucca suds.

Treatment in dye: Bring to boiling point slowly and boil gently
   from 1-2 hours. Liquid will slowly lose brilliancy. Add ½ cup
   (150 ml.) sumac berry liquid. Dye reaches stable phase.

After treatment: Remove from dye, wring slightly and dry. Rinse
   thoroughly.

Result: Wool, a good, deep maroon; cotton, a good pink.

Washing test: Wool, fairly fast, slightly more bluish; cotton not
   fast, turns blue.

Test No. 1
   Use Stock Dye No. 1 and Recipe No. 12.
   Substitute unwashed wool and cotton which has been soaked
   in liquid sheep manure. (See Chapter V.)

Result: Wool, a good, deep maroon; cotton, a good pink.

Washing test: Wool, permanent; cotton, turns bluish.

Test No. 2
   Use Stock Dye No. 1 and Recipe No. 12.
   Substitute cotton washed and boiled a few minutes in plain
   water. Immerse in dye. Soak 48 hours.

Result: Cotton, before rinsing, a very fine, brilliant maroon; turns
   more bluish when rinsed.

Washing test: Not fast, will not stand soap.

Test No. 3
   Use Stock Dye No. 1 and Recipe No. 12.

After treatment: When wool or cotton is removed from dye and wrung out, place at once in smoker. (See Chapter V.) Smoke about 10 minutes. Wool slightly darkened. Rinse thoroughly.

Result: Wool, good, dark maroon.

Washing test: Wool, fast; cotton, turns bluish.

Recipe No. 13   PURPLE CORN   For wool and cotton
                                  KOKO'MA BROWN
                          koko'ma (Zea mays amylacea)

Use Stock Dye No. 2.

Mordanting: Add to Stock Dye No. 2, ½ cup (150 ml.) of liquid from sumac berries, produced by boiling berries ½ hour or soaked 24 hours. 1 handful (20-25 grams) of berries in 1-1/3 cups (300 ml.) of water. Strain berries through cloth and squeeze out juice. Replace on fire. Boil down to about 6 cups (1½ litres).

Material added: To 6 cups (1½ litres) of this dye add 1 double handful (30-40 grams) of wool or cotton washed in yucca suds, then rinsed.

Treatment in dye: Bring to boiling point slowly and boil for 1-2 hours.

After treatment: Remove from dye, wring lightly and dry, then rinse thoroughly.

Result: Wool, a good, red-brown; cotton, fair.

Washing test: Wool, fairly fast, loses a little color; cotton, fair.

Recipe No. 14   PURPLE CORN   For wool and cotton
                                   KOKO'MA TAN
                           koko'ma (Zea mays amylacea)
Use Stock Dye No. 1.

Mordanting: Add ¾ cup (200 ml.) of sumac berry liquid; then add 1 handful (25 ml.) of ground native alum.

Material added: To 6 cups (1½ litres) of this dye add 1 double handful (30-40 grams) of wool or cotton washed in yucca suds and rinsed, then boiled with alum.

Treatment in dye: Immerse in dye, and bring to boiling point slowly. Boil 2 hours.

After treatment: Remove from dye, wring lightly and dry. Rinse thoroughly.

Result: Wool, a dull pink-brown or tan; cotton, good pink-tan. Note: If a second dip is required, the pan may be set upon the stove and reheated but it must not be allowed to boil.

Test No. 1

Use Stock Dye No. 1 and Recipe No. 14.

Preparation of material: Substitute wool washed in yucca and rinsed.

Treatment in dye: Immerse in dye, boil for 2 hours.

Result: Wool, light pink-tan.

Recipe No. 15   PURPLE CORN   For wool and cotton
                       KOKO'MA BLUE
                   koko'ma (Zea mays amylacea)

Use Stock Dye No. 1.

Mordanting: Add ¼ cup (200 ml.) of sumac berry liquid. Liquid is intensified in color.

Material added: To 6 cups (1½ litres) of this dye add 1 double handful (30-40 grams) of wool washed in Lux soap and rinsed or cotton boiled in plain water.

Treatment in dye: Bring to boiling point slowly and remove from fire.

After treatment: Set aside and soak for 48 hours. Remove from dye, wring slightly and dry. Rinse thoroughly.

Result: Wool, a good blue; cotton, same.

Washing test: Wool, loses color; cotton, same.

CHAPTER XI

Greens

Vegetable dyes in which *two* colors are used to produce *one* shade

THE WRITER'S EXPERIMENTS and research have proved that two separate colors cannot be mixed together in the same dye pot, to produce a third color, such as yellow plus blue equals green, or blue plus red equals purple.

Provided a plant cannot be used which will produce the desired color in one operation such colors must then be produced in the following manner.

The two colors necessary to produce the third color are prepared in separate dye pots and the material, wool, cotton or basketry fibers, are dyed first in one color and then in the other. Thus the colors are *superimposed* one upon another, avoiding chemical reactions.

The resulting shades are clear and strong.

The material dyed, whatever it may be, must be allowed to dry before its immersion in the second dye.

After the material is dry and when it is ready to dip in the second color, it should first be soaked in warm water and lightly wrung out, then the material will take the dye more evenly. When used in a "two dye" process, indigo dye may be slightly warmed.

The recipes for "greens" in this paper are produced as described above.

Recipe No. 1   RABBIT BRUSH & INDIGO   For wool and cotton
YELLOW ON BLUE
(Siva'pi Green and Indigo)

Use Indigo Blue Recipe No. 1.

Use Siva'pi Yellow Stock Dye No. 1.

Mordanting: Add to 8 cups of *siva'pi* yellow dye 1 small double handful (100 ml.) of ground alum. This mixture foams and the liquid turns opaque yellow.

Material added: To 8 cups (2 litres) of this dye add ½ hank of indigo dyed wool or cotton yarn soaked in warm water before immersing in dye.

Treatment in dye: Immerse in dye, bring to boil slowly and boil about 1 hour.

After treatment: Color is improved by soaking wool or cotton in dye overnight after boiling. Remove from dye, wring lightly and dry. Rinse thoroughly.

Result: A good, even, deep green.

Remarks: No yellow float which may be prevented by the overnight soaking.

Recipe No. 2   RABBIT BRUSH & INDIGO   For wool
YELLOW ON BLUE (alternate)
(Siva'pi Green and Indigo)

Use Indigo Blue Recipe No. 1.

Use Siva'pi Yellow Stock Dye No. 1.

Mordanting: Add to Siva'pi Yellow Stock Dye No. 1 (alternate) 1 small double handful (100 ml.) of ground native alum — mixture foams.

Material added: To 4 cups (1 litre) of this dye add about 1 small handful or ½ hank (20 grams) of spun yarn dyed in Indigo Blue Recipe No. 1. This should be first soaked in warm water for a few moments to remove air bubbles before immersing in the *siva'pi* dye.

Treatment in dye: Immerse in dye, bring to boiling point slowly and boil 1 hour.

After treatment: Remove from dye, wring thoroughly and dry. Rinse well in warm water after drying.

Result: Wool, a good, dark green, but yellow overlay on blue quite evident.

RABBIT BRUSH
Recipe No. 3   & INDIGO   For wool and cotton
BLUE ON YELLOW
(Siva'pi and Indigo Green)

Use Siva'pi Yellow Stock Dye No. 1.

Use Recipes Nos. 1 or 2 and Indigo Blue Recipe No. 1.

Mordanting: Take 1 large double handful (50 grams) of dyed *siva'pi* yellow wool.

Material added: Soak in lukewarm water, wring lightly and immerse in indigo blue dye pot.

Treatment in dye: Stir thoroughly and treat as in Indigo Blue Recipe No. 1. Soak from 12 to 48 hours, depending upon the shade of green desired. Shades from a gold-green to a deep, blue-green can be produced, depending upon the period of immersion.

After treatment: Remove, wring lightly and dry in the open air. Rinse thoroughly after drying.

Result: Wool, a good green; cotton, fair. The blue of the indigo superimposed upon the yellow of the *siva'pi* produces fine shades of green. (This is the preferred method.) The reverse process shows film of imposed yellow on the indigo, (except when soaked overnight). Indigo dye should never be boiled.

RABBIT BRUSH & INDIGO   For basketry (wicker)
GREEN
(Siva'pi Green and Indigo)

Wicker basketry material may be successfully dyed green by immersing first in *siva'pi* yellow dye, and later in a bath of indigo blue. (If the process is reversed, there will be a "float" of yellow on the dyed indigo. For one exception, see Recipe No. 1, Yellow on Blue.)

1. Yellow dye bath

For this purpose allow the material to dry before dyeing in indigo. If desired, it can be smoked while still damp (see smoking), and then dyed in indigo. (See recipe "Siva'pi Indigo.")

2. Indigo dye bath

The indigo dye is *not heated*. The basketry material is immersed in the cool dye and handled just as it is described above for *siva'pi* yellow. When finished, this color is *not smoked*.

3. *Saqwa* — Indigo dip — light green*

Dip basketry material in indigo and soak and then smoke this with white wool and flowers of *siva'pi*.
Result: Light green.
If you use same recipe with dark wool — dark green.

* This recipe was not tested by the writer.

RABBIT BRUSH & BLUE KIDNEY BEAN   For basketry
SIVA'PI AND TUPENMORI — GREEN
(*Chrysothamnus* sp. and *Phaseolus vulgaris*)

Basketry material dyed as in Siva'pi Yellow Recipe No. 1. Place this dyed material in the blue dye of the blue-black bean, and remove when turning green.

Place at once in a smoker. If this material does not become green enough when smoked, dip in dye again and smoke once more.
Result: A nice, apple-green.

The *siva'pi* yellow basket material must *not* be allowed to boil in hot bean dye; simply heated and then removed from stove. If allowed to boil, the yellow will boil out before the blue has time to penetrate.

CHAPTER XII

Blacks

THERE ARE TWO PRINCIPAL ways of making black dye and, of course, there are individual minor variations in these methods. Both recipes are given, although the chemical principle is the same in each.

In both cases, the chief factors are iron and tannin, which together produce a blue-black ink or dye.

In both recipes the insoluble yellow ochre or (limonite) iron hydroxide is reduced to a soluble form by burning the ore with gum of the pinyon tree. This process produces a fine black soot or powder which is soluble in water.

The tannin is produced in two forms:

(1) From the seeds of the black seeded Indian sunflower *(Helianthus* sp.).

(2) From the leaves and branchlets of *su:'vi*, or sumac *(Rhus trilobata).*

How the intricate chemical principle involved in this process was discovered by the Hopi, and probably by other tribes of the Southwest,* will always remain an intriguing mystery.

Cotton, wool and basketry materials are all dyed with these dyes.

When "Sunflower Seed — Iron Black" is used, natural black or brown wool is always used instead of white, as the shade of black produced on this is more intense.

Cotton does not take this dye well. Basketry material, however, can be dyed a good blue-black.

The black-seeded sunflower is a cultivated plant, it is grown in

---

* Also used by Navajo (Bryan and Young, 1940, pp. 65-67).

northern Arizona at an altitude of about 4,500 feet, in semi-desert country.

"Sumac — Iron Black" is usually dyed on dark wool and this dye will also dye cotton a good black. It is successful on basketry material.

SUNFLOWER SEED & YELLOW OCHRE   For basketry
(a) BLACK
'A:'qaw'u or Sunflower Seed (*Helianthus* sp.) and
Yellow Ochre (iron hydroxide)

(b) BLACK OR BLUE
SUMAC *su:'vi* or Sumac (*Rhus trilobata*) and Iron

Both methods of producing black dye can be used successfully on basketry material, both wicker and yucca types.

Dyeing

The mordanted dye is allowed to cool until nearly lukewarm, in a receptacle long and deep enough to accommodate the length of the material (10-15 inches). The stems or strips are immersed in this dye bath either loose or tied lightly in bundles. The vessel is gently agitated at intervals and the bundles turned so that the dye will take evenly on the material.

Black basketry material is not smoked after dyeing.

Stock Dye No. 1

(a) BLACK

(iron, ·from pinyon gum and yellow ochre (iron hydroxide)
and sunflower seed *(Helianthus* sp.*)*

Part 1

Take lumps of pinyon gum as free of dirt as possible. Melt in
an iron pan or kettle and strain through a cloth or fine sieve.
Prepare this outdoors. (The Hopi strained pinyon gum through
coarse horse tail hair, etc.) Replace melted gum in a long-
handled iron frying pan and bring to boil. This should be done
over a fire outdoors also, as this smoke injures the throat.

Melted gum — about 2 cups (400 ml.). Grind about 1 large
double handful (150 ml.) of lump ochre (limonite) to powder
on a stone mortar, a little at a time. Add this powder to the
boiling pinyon gum and stir constantly until the mass darkens
and thickens. Allow the mixture to boil down or to "catch fire,"
and continue to stir with a long stick. In 15 or 20 minutes the
mass will blacken and turn crisp. Remove from fire, and grind
charred mass to fine, black powder on a stone mortar.

Result: Thus the iron in the limonite or ochre has now been reduced to a form soluble in water.

Part 2

Take purple sunflower seed — 1 large double handful (150 ml.).
Water — 8 cups (2 litres). Bring to boil slowly. Boil gently ½
hour or until seeds begin to crack open. Remove from fire
and strain.

Result: Deep, reddish-purple liquid.

Part 3

Add to this about 1 small double handful (100 ml.) of ground
native alum. Dye liquid at once turns a deep, blue-purple.
Now add to this liquid 1 small double handful (100 ml.) of
the oxide-pinyon gum powder. Stir well and boil ½ hour.

Result: This dye should be a fine, rich blue-black ink. The principle
of the gum-ochre powder is iron, which forms an ink when
combined with the tannin in the sunflower dye.

Stock Dye No. 2
(b) BLACK
su:'vi (Rhus trilobata) and limonite
(Pinyon gum, yellow ochre and sumac)
Part 1

Fill a 4-quart kettle with the crushed branchlets and leaves of sumac. Boil slowly about 4 hours, when the tannin in this liquid will be very strong.

Part 2

Prepare pinyon gum and yellow ochre as in Black (a). To 6 cups (1½ litres) of this liquid from the sumac branches, add about 80 grams of pinyon gum powder. The liquid at once turns to a black ink. Boil for a few minutes, and add brown or black wool, or cotton. Boil 3-4 hours. Remove, wring out, dry and rinse thoroughly.

Result: Wool, a good black; cotton, similar.*

---

* The Navajo use the same method to obtain a good black (Bryan and Young, 1940, pp. 65-67).

Recipe No. 1   For wool and cotton
BLACK
Sunflower Seed *(Helianthus* sp.*)* and Yellow Ochre
Use Stock Dye No. 1.

Material added: To 6 cups (1½ litres) of this dye, add 1 double handful (40 grams) of dark brown or black wool (never white) washed in yucca suds.

Treatment in dye: Bring to boil slowly, and boil gently 4 hours, stirring frequently.

After treatment: Remove, wring out slightly and dry. Rinse thoroughly, after drying.

Result: Wool, a fine blue-black; cotton, when treated with this dye, produces a dirty gray.

Recipe No. 2   For wool
BLACK
Sunflower Seed *(Helianthus* sp.) and Yellow Ochre

Use Stock Dye No. 1.

Mordanting: Add to this liquid 1 small double handful (100 ml.) of ground native alum. Dye at once turns a deep blue-purple.

Material added: To 6 cups (1½ litres) of this dye, add 1 double handful (40 grams) of wool or cotton. Use unwashed wool from which the dirt has been shaken out. Fill a quart jar with juniper ashes; then pour into the jar as much water as it will hold. Let this settle overnight. Pour off in morning, and in this liquid soak wool which has been dyed. This will set the color.

Recipe No. 3   For wool
BLACK (jet) and BLUE (pale)
'A:'qaw'u — Sunflower Seed *(Helianthus* sp.)

Pinyon gum, 3 to 5 pounds. Boil down pinyon gum in a pot, add sulphur powder which is found in association with native coal. Stir constantly until the mass becomes dusty dry. Sunflower seed *('a:'qaw'u)* is boiled down and strained. The pinyon gum and sulphur mixture is added and the mixture is again boiled.

Result: This produces a jet black dye, which, if used diluted, will make a gray-blue dye.

Amsden, Charles Avery
1934 *Navaho Weaving, Its Technic and Its History*
Santa Ana, California: The Fine Arts Press

Bartlett, Katharine
1950 *Present Trends in Weaving on the Western Navaho Reservation*
Plateau, vol. 23, no. 1. Museum of Northern Arizona, Flagstaff

Bennett, Noël
1974 *The Weaver's Pathway: A Clarification of 'The Spirit Trail' in Navajo Weaving*
Flagstaff, Arizona: Northland Press

Bennett, Noël and Bighorse, Tiana
1971 *Working with Wool*
Flagstaff, Arizona: Northland Press

Berlant, Anthony and Kahlenberg, Mary Hunt
1972 *The Navajo Blanket*
New York: Praeger Publications, Inc.
1977 *Walk in Beauty: The Navajos and Their Blankets*
Boston: New York Graphic Society

Bliss, Anne
1976 *Rocky Mountain Dye Plants*
Boulder, Colorado: Johnson Printing Co.

Boyd, Dorothy Elizabeth
1970 *Navajo Pictorial Weaving: Its Past and Its Present Condition*
Unpublished M.A. Thesis, University of New Mexico

Brody, J.J.
1976 *Between Traditions: Navajo Weaving Toward the End of the Nineteenth Century*
Iowa City: Stamats Publishing Co.

Bryan, Nonobah G.
1978 *Navajo Native Dyes: Their Preparation and Use*
Palmer Lake, Colorado: Filter Press

Cerny, Charlene
1975 *Navajo Pictorial Weaving*
Santa Fe: Museum of New Mexico Foundation

Colton, M.R.F.   88
    1932 *Wool for Our Indian Weavers – What Shall It Be?*
          Museum Notes, vol. 4, no. 12: Museum of Northern Arizona, Flagstaff

Dedera, Don
    1975 *Navajo Rugs: How to Find, Evaluate, Buy and Care for Them*
          Flagstaff, Arizona: Northland Press

Dockstader, Frederick J.
    1978 *Weaving Arts of the North American Indians*
          New York: Thomas Y. Crowell

Douglas, Frederic H.
    1951 *Navaho Wearing Blankets*
          Leaflet #113: Department of Indian Art, Denver Art Museum, Denver
    1953 *Southwestern Weaving Materials*
          Leaflet #116: Department of Indian Art, Denver Art Museum, Denver

Dutton, Bertha
    1961 *Navaho Weaving Today*
          Santa Fe: Museum of New Mexico Press

Gilpin, Laura
    1968 *The Enduring Navaho*
          Austin Texas: University of Texas Press

James, George Wharton
    1914 *Indian Blankets and Their Makers*
          Chicago: A.C. McClory & Co.
          (also in paperback, 1974, New York: Dover Publications, Inc.)

Kent, Kate Peck
    1957 *The Cultivation and Weaving of Cotton in the Prehistoric
          Southwestern United States*
          Trans. of the A.P.S. n.s. vol. 47, part 3, pp. 457-732. American
          Philosophical Society, Philadelphia
    1961 *The Story of Navaho Weaving*
          Phoenix: Heard Museum

Matthews, Washington
    1968 *Navajo Weavers, Navajo Silversmiths*
          Palmer Lake, Colorado: Filter Press
          (Reprinted from the 3rd annual BAE Report, 1881.)

Maxwell, Gilbert
    1963 *Navaho Rugs*
       Palm Desert, California: Best West Publications
Mera, H.P.
    1947 *Navaho Textile Arts*
       Santa Fe: Laboratory of Anthropology

Mera, H.P. and Moss, Roger and Jean
    1975 *Navaho Textile Arts*
       Santa Barbara, Califorina and Salt Lake City, Utah: Peregrine-Smith, Inc.

Mera, H.P. and Wheat, Joe Ben
    1978 *The Alfred I. Barton Collection of Southwest Textiles*
       Miami, Florida: The Lowe Art Museum

Museum of New Mexico
    1977 *Navajo Weaving Handbook*
       Santa Fe: Museum of New Mexico Press

Reichard, Gladys A.
    1974 *Weaving a Navajo Blanket*
       New York: Dover Publications
       (First published as Navajo Shepherd and Weaver, 1936)
    1936 *Navaho Sheep and Weavers*
       New York: J.J. Augustin

Rodee, Marian E.
    1977 *Southwestern Weaving*
       Albuquerque: University of New Mexico Press
    1981 *Old Navajo Rugs, Their Development from 1900-1940*
       Albuquerque: University of New Mexico Press

Spier, Leslie
    1924 *Zuñi Weaving Technique*
       American Anthropologist #26 pp. 64-85

Underhill, Ruth M.
    1956 *The Navajos*
       Norman, Oklahoma: University of Oklahoma Press

Wheat, Joe Ben
    1974 *Three Centuries of Navajo Weaving*
       Arizona Highways, July issue, pp 13, 22-23, 34, 42-45
    1976 *Navajo Textiles in the Fred Harvey Fine Arts Collection*
       Phoenix: Heard Museum

Whiting, A.F.

1939 *Ethnobotany of the Hopi*

Bulletin #15, Northern Arizona Society of Science and Art, Inc.,
Flagstaff

Bill Rieske
HISTORIC INDIAN PUBLISHERS
1404 Sunset Drive
P.O. Box 16074
Salt Lake City, Utah 84116-0074